# THE BEST OF
# ROBERT BURNS
## IN ENGLISH

# THE BEST OF ROBERT BURNS
## IN ENGLISH

## William Curran

FOREWORD BY
### Sir Samuel Curran
*Principal and Vice-Chancellor*
*Strathclyde University 1964–80*

## The Book Guild Ltd
### Sussex, England

*To my dear wife*
*Dorothy Mary Curran, née Ord*
*and her Scottish forbears*

---

The Book Guild Limited
25/26 High Street
Lewes, Sussex

First published 1990
© William Curran 1990

Set in Baskerville
Typeset by Central Southern
Typesetters, Eastbourne

Made and printed in Great Britain
By Antony Rowe Ltd
Chippenham, Wiltshire

British Library Cataloguing in Publication Data
The best of Robert Burns in English.
I. Curran, William *1913–* II. Burns, Robert *1757–1796*
821'.6

ISBN 0 86332 451 7

# CONTENTS

## FOREWORD BY SIR SAMUEL CURRAN
### Principal and Vice-Chancellor
### Strathclyde University 1964–80

I should say that I am not related to the author, Mr William Curran. We came to know each other simply because we carried the same name. When I learned that he had translation into English of many of the works of Burns in mind I expressed keen interest. I had appreciated for a long time the great need for such translation of most of the poetry of Burns into English, the most widespread language of the present-day world. As Principal and Vice-Chancellor of Strathclyde University I had need and opportunity to visit different parts of the world and so came to realise the extent to which Burns was truly a world figure.

To illustrate this world-wide renown of Burns, I was invited by a senior government minister to meetings with leaders in science of the USSR. At a dinner in Novosibirsk a number of us made short speeches and I came last of five in the British party to speak. Much had been said about the world fellowship that science could create but in my remarks I expressed fear that science could divide as well as unite. I proceeded to quote from 'For all that and all that' to illustrate fellowship as visualised by Burns. This was received extremely well, particularly considering no translation into English was made. Most of the Soviet scientists were obviously familiar with Burns and my neighbour at table, a leading world figure in applied mathematics, wrote down from memory the numbers of six long playing records of Burns that were available in Russian. He wanted me to buy them. I thought then that it was most unlikely such an incident could occur in London which likes to see itself as a world centre of culture. It is too easy to overlook the riches near home!

I trust this work of translation of much of Burns will help to bring his great contributions into the minds of many English-speaking people. It is to be hoped that the volume will prove very valuable to many in England and also to

Americans, Canadians and Australians. Even though I have lived much of my life in Scotland I have difficulty in grasping the meaning of the words of the Scots dialect that flowed so smoothly and with so much feeling and sensibility from the pen of Burns but which are now used less and less in every-day life in South-West Scotland. We are trying now to devise a 'caring society' but Burns was more than two hundred years ahead of us in this effort. He deserves all the esteem that application such as that of the author brings to his cause. I feel a real gap is being filled by publication of this work and I do hope it proves a blessing to a great many new followers of the poet.

# PREFACE

Many have denied themselves the pleasure of reading and understanding the works of Robert Burns because of his combination of English with a Scottish dialect; there being too many distractions when referring to the copious foot-notes or glossary (perforce some have been used). It is to remedy this that this 'translation' is offered.

Robert was the first born (1759) of a family of independent yeoman stock. His father, who made a frugal living farming inferior land, died in 1784 leaving him the mainstay of the family. He published his first poems in 1786, married in 1788, and obtained a post in the Excise in 1789 which he held till his death in 1796 at the age of 37. On his death bed he was tormented by a debt of £15 and in the knowledge his wife was about to be confined. This financial embarrassment could so easily have been avoided had he accepted payment for the generous contributions he was making to two National publications, and the offer of a retainer from a London political newspaper; or had he heeded the advice of his learned friend and correspondent Dr. Moore*:-

It is evident that you already possess a great variety of expression and command of the English language; you ought therefore deal more sparingly, for the future, in the provincial dialect – why should you, by using that, limit the number of admirers to those who understand the Scottish, when you could extend it to all persons of taste who understand the English language.

vide, The Works of Robert Burns, vol. 1V Blackie & sons (1887)

His poems and songs, which are here treated the same, are also chronicles of his times. Biographers and editions of his works are legion, but in spite of such a close scrutiny of them one is looking for a more profound reason how, from such an inauspicious background, he has left such a legacy. His

*Father of General Sir John Moore of Corunna

meagre informal education was paid for in pennies scraped from the tightest of family budgets. He studied and composed in a spartan environment overburdened with filial cares and duties, yet he excelled in English, absorbed some French together with Greek mythology, and knew his bible thoroughly.

He was well acquainted with current affairs and world politics (which were then in pretty much the same state as they are today). He had a wide circle of friends, was well connected, and was by no means a peasant poet. Initially he was lauded by cultural Edinburgh and the 'Establishment' which diminished because of his outspoken liberal views.

Essentially, he was a human and humane poet, expressing with beauty perceptive observations on 'The lowly train in life's sequestered scene' He bestowed immortality on all living things; mice and men, dogs and daisies, sheep and horses, all appear in his allegories. He is never more eloquent than in his poems and songs to the fairer sex, 'our dearest blessing here below'.

There were many diversions in his private life, the consequences of which he suffered in full, asking only:-

> Gently scan your fellow man,
> More gently your sister woman,
> Although they know they're doing wrong,
> To step aside is human.

'Translations' are such as to warrant that neither the sense or the sentiments have suffered, comparative examples are given in the appendix.

# TAM O'SHANTER

Acknowledged to be Burns' greatest work. Thomas of Shanter Farm, returning home in a bemused state on a wild winter's night, disturbs the incumbents of Alloway churchyard at their midnight revels. Fleeing before them, Nannie the comeliest and swiftest in her cutty sark (short shirt), divests Tam's mare of its tail.

When winter darkness clears the street,
And thirsty neighbours neighbours meet,
As market days are wearing late,
And folk begin to take the gate;
While we sit boozing at the nappy,                    *Ale.*
And getting drunk and oh so happy,
We think not on the long Scots miles,
Mosses, waters, fields and stiles,
That lie between us and our hame,
Where sits our sulky, sullen dame,
Gathering her brows like a gathering storm,
Nursing her wrath to keep it warm.

This truth found honest Tam O' Shanter,
As he from Ayr one night did canter.
(Old Ayr that ne'er a town surpasses
For honest men and bonny lasses.)

O Tam had thou but been so wise,
As to take your own wife Kate's advice.
She told you well you were a waster,
A blethering, blustering, bloated boaster;
That from November till October,
On market days you ne'er were sober,
That with the money from the miller,
You drank as long as you had silver;
From every horse he put a shoe on,
The smith and thee got roaring drunk on;
That after prayers, even on Sunday,

You drank with Kirkton Jean till Monday.     *Innkeeper.*
She prophesised that late or soon,
Thou wouldst be found deep drowned in Doon;
Or caught by warlocks in the mirk,
By Alloway's old haunted kirk.

Ah, gentle dames, it makes me greet,     *Cry.*
To think how many counsels sweet,
How many lengthened sage advices,
The husband from the wife despises.

But to our tale:— one market night,
Tam was planted snug and tight,
Close by a fire burning brightly,
With foaming ale that drank divinely
And at his elbow cobbler Johnnie,
His ancient, trusty, thirsty crony;
Tam loved him like a very brother;
They had been drunk for weeks together.
The night drew on with songs and clatter;
And aye the ale was growing better;
The landlady and Tam grew gracious;
With favours secret, sweet and precious,
The cobbler told his queerest stories;
The landlord's laugh was ready chorus:
The storm without might roar and rustle,
Tam did'nt mind the storm a whistle.

Care, mad to see a man so happy,
Even drowned itself amongst the nappy.     *Ale.*
As bees fly home with loads of treasure,
The minutes winged their way with pleasure:
Kings may be blessed but Tam was glorious,
Over all the ills of life victorious.

But pleasures are like poppies spread,
You seize the flower, its bloom is shed;
Just like a snowflake in the river,
A moment white – then melts forever;
Or like the fleeting Northern Lights
That flit before your very sights;

Or like the rainbow's lovely form
Evanishing amid the storm.
No man can tether Time nor Tide;
The hour approaches, Tam must ride –
That hour, of night's black arch the keystone,
That dreary hour he mounts his beast in;
And such a night he takes the road in,
As ne'er poor sinner was abroad in.

The wind blew as if it blew its last;
The rattling showers rose on the blast,
The speedy gleams the darkness swallowed;
Loud, deep, and long, the thunder bellowed:
That night, a child might understand,
The Devil had business on his hand.

Well mounted on his grey mare, Meg,
A better never lifted leg,
Tam cantered on through mud and mire,
Despising wind, and rain, and fire;
Whiles holding fast his good blue bonnet:
Whiles crooning o'er an old Scots sonnet;
Whiles glowering round with prudent cares,
Lest bogies catch him unawares;
Alloway church was drawing nigh,
Where ghosts and owlets nightly cry.

By this time he was across the ford,
Where in the snow a man was smothered;
And past the big dark standing stones,
Where drunken Charlie broke his bones;
Then through the whins and by the cairn,
Where hunters found the murdered bairn;
And near the thorn, above the well,
Where Mungo's mother hanged hersel'.
Before him Doon pours all its floods;
The doubling storm roars through the woods;
The lightnings flash from pole to pole;
Near and more near the thunders roll;
When, glimmering through the groaning trees,
Alloway church seemed in a bleeze;                    *blaze.*

Through every space the gleams were glancing;
And loud resounding mirth and dancing.

Inspiring old John Barleycorn, *Ale.*
What dangers you can make us scorn,
With twopenny ale we fear no evil;
With whisky raw we'll face the devil.
The drink so roamed in Tammie's noddle,
Fair play he cared not for a boddle. *Small coin.*
But Maggie stood right sore astonished,
Till by the heel and hand admonished,
She ventured forward on the light,
And, wow, Tam saw a frightful sight.

Warlocks and witches in a dance;
No fancy stuff brand new from France,
But hornpipes, jigs, strathspeys, and reels;
Put life and mettle in their heels.
At the window in the east,
There sat old Nick in shape of beast; *Devil.*
A black hound dog both grim and large,
To give them music was his charge:
He blew the pipes with such a skill,
Rafters re-echoed at his will.
Coffins stood round like open presses, *Cupboards.*
That showed the dead in their last dresses;
And by some devilish tricky slight,
Each in its cold hand held a light,
By which heroic Tam was able
To note upon the holy table, *Altar.*
A murderer's bones in gibbet irons;
Two span-long wee unchristened bairns;
A thief, new cutted from a rape,
With his last gasp his mouth did gape;
Five tomahawks, with blood red-rusted;
Five scimitars, with murder crusted;
A garter which a babe had strangled;
A knife a father's throat had mangled,
Whom his own son of life bereft,
The grey hairs yet stuck to the heft *Handle.*
There was more, more horrible and awful,
Which even to mention would be unlawful.

As Tammie gazed, amazed and curious,
The mirth and fun grew fast and furious.
The piper loud and louder blew;
The dancers quick and quicker flew.
They reeled, they crossed, they locked, they set,
Till every wraith was wet with sweat,
And threw their clothes into the dark,
Each tripping in their flannel sark.                              *Shirt.*


Now Tam, O Tam, had they been queans,
All plump and strapping in their teens;
Their shirts, instead of itching flannel,
Been snowy white new-laundered linen;
These pants of mine, my only pair,
That once were plush with good blue hair,
I would have given them off my hurdies,                      *Thighs.*
For one blink of the bonnie birdies.


But, withered witches, old and droll,
Hade's hags that could wean a foal,
Jumping and flinging on their crummocks,                    *Staffs.*
Enough to turn stout Scottish stomachs.

But Tam knew what was what all right;
Espied a wench a winsome sight,
That night enlisted in the corps,
(Long after known on rocky shores:
For many a beast to dead she shot,
And perished many a bonnie boat,
And ruined crops both far and near,
And kept the countryside in fear).
Her cutty sark of paisley harn,              *Short shirt. Coarse cloth.*
That while a lassie she had worn,
In longtitude though sorely scanty,
It was her best and she was jaunty.
Ah: little thought thy reverend grannie,
The shirt she bought for her wee Nannie,
With two pounds Scotch ('twas all her riches),
Would ever grace a dance of witches.

But here my muse must go much slower;
Such flights are far beyond her power;
To see how Nannie leapt along,
(A supple jade she was and strong)
And how Tam stood, like one bewitched,
And thought his very eye enriched;
Even Satan glowered, and fumed in vain,
And huffed and blew with might and main;
Till first one caper then another,
Tam lost his reason altogether
And roars out, 'Well done, Cutty Sark'.          *Short shirt.*
And in an instant all was dark:
And scarcely had he Maggie rallied,
When out the hellish legion sallied.
As bees buzz out on vengeful wings;
Mauling marauders with their stings,
As dogs asleep with one eye closed,
A cat appears before their nose;
As eager runs the market crowd,
When 'Catch the thief' resounds aloud;
So Maggie runs, the witches follow,
With many a curdling screech and holler.

Oh, Tam, Oh Tam, you'll get your fairing;          *Deserts.*
In hell they'll roast thee like a herring;
In vain thy Kate awaits thy coming,
Kate soon will be a woeful woman.
Now, do thy utmost sturdy Meg,
And win the keystone of the bridge;
There at them your tail you may toss,
A running stream they dare not cross.
But ere the keystone she could make,
Her only tail she had to shake,
For Nannie, far before the rest,
Hard upon noble Maggie pressed,
And flew at Tam in furious fettle,
But little knew she Maggie's mettle.
One spring brought off her master hale,          *Whole.*
But left behind her own gray tail:
For Nannie caught her by the rump,
And left poor Maggie scarce a stump.

Now who this tale of truth shall read,
Every man and mother's son take heed,
Whenever to drink you are inclined,
And cutty sarks run in your mind,                    *Fast women.*
Think, you may but the joys overdear,
Remember Tam O' Shanter's mare.


It is a well known fact that witches or any evil spirits have no power to follow a poor wight any further than the next running stream. It may be proper likewise to mention to the benighted traveller, that, when he falls in with bogies, whatever danger there may be in his going forward, there is much more hazard in going back.                              R.B.

## TO A YOUNG LADY

Who was looking up the text of a castigating sermon.

Fair maid, you need not take the hint,
Nor idle texts pursue,
It was guilty sinners that he meant,
Not angels such as you.

## THE INVENTORY

The local tax collector, a Mr. Aiken, had required of Burns a detailed list of all his possessions.

Sir, as your mandate did request,
I send you here a faithful list
Of goods and gear, of each and both,
To which I hereby give my oath.

First of all for carriage cattle,                    *Horses.*
I have four brutes of gallant mettle,
As ever went before a pettle.                        *Plough.*
My left hand fore's a good old has-been,
Both long and faithful has his days been;
My left hand rear's a well-bred filly,
That oft has brought me home from Killie,            *Kilmarnock.*
From Mauchline too so many a time,
In days when riding was no crime:
But once, when in my wooing pride,
I, like a blockhead, chose to ride,
The wilful creature I so spurred,
I craved a pardon from the Lord.
For my riding was so very craven,
She's now bedevilled with the spavin.
My right hand rear's a worthy beast
As ever in plough or cart was traced.
The fourth's proved me a simple fool,
It's dammed stark mad, just like a mule.
Forbye a colt, of colts the best,
Each task he does with zeal and zest.
If he be spared to be a horse,
He'll earn for me a tidy purse.

Wheel carriages I have but few,
Three carts, and two are nearly new;
An old wheelbarrow, more for token;
One leg and both the shafts are broken;
I made a poker of the spindle,
And my old mother burnt the trundle.                 *Wheel.*

For men, I've three mischievous boys,
Small devils for shouting and for noise;
A ploughboy one, a thresher the other,
Wee Davie feeds the cattle fodder.
I rule them, as I ought, discreetly,
And often labour them completely:
Always on Sundays duly, nightly
I on the Bible ask them tightly;
Till, faith, wee Davies turned so gleg,          *Clever.*
Though scarcely longer than my leg,
He'll reel you off the catechism,
As fast as any in the dwelling,

I've none in female serving station,
(Lord, keep me always from temptation).
I have no wife my life to laden,
And you have never taxed a maiden;
And then, if churchfolk do not touch me,
I know the Devil will not clutch me.
With babes I'm more than well-contented,
Heaven sent me one more than I wanted,
My comely smirking dear bought Bess,          *Illegitimate.*
She stares the daddy in her face,
Enough of ought you like but grace;
But her, my bonnie sweet wee lady,
I've paid enough for her already,
And if you tax her or her mother,
By Lord, you'll get them both together.

And now remember Mr. Aiken,
No kind of licence out I'm taking;
From this time forth I do declare,
Mare or maid I'll ride no more;
Through muck and mire all life I'll paddle,
E're I would pay so dear for a saddle;
My travels all on foot I'll walk it,
I've sturdy bearers, God be thankit,          *Legs.*
The Church and you'll take all I've got,
It puts but little in your pot;
So do not put me in your book,
Nor for my ten white shillings look.

This list with my own hand I've wrote it,
The day and date as undernoted,
Then know all ye whom it concerns,
*Subscripsi huic*      Robert Burns.


Mossgiel, February 22, 1786.

## LAST MAY A BRAW WOOER
### (Last May A Fine Fellow)

Last May a fine fellow came down the long glen,
So intense was his love that he won me;
I said there was nothing I hated like men,
The Devil take him, he believed me.

He spoke of the darts in my bonnie black een,                    *Eyes*
And vowed for my love he was dying,
I said he might die when he liked for his Jean;
The Lord forgive me for lying.

A well-furnished farm with him for its Laird,
And marriage offhand were his proffers;
I never let on that I knew or cared,
But I thought I might get better offers.

But what do you think? In two weeks or less,
(I'm surprised that he ever went near her)
He went up the glen to black cousin Bess,
The jade, I could never abide her.

But all the next week as I fretted with care,
I went to the town of Dalgarnock,
And who but my fine fickle lover was there?
I glowered as I'd seen a warlock.

But o'er my left shoulder I gave him a wink,
Lest neighbours might say I was saucy,
My lover he capered as he'd been in drink,
And vowed I was his dear lassie.

I asked 'bout my cousin, in a sweet tender way,
And if she'd recovered her hearing,
And if her new shoes fit her big awkward feet,
But heavens, how he fell a swearing.

He begged for God's sake I would be his wife,
Or else I would kill him with sorrow,
And so to preserve the poor body his life,
I think I will wed him tomorrow.

## THE TWA DOGS

Two dogs, one of gentle birth, the other of more humble, hold a dissertation on the social differences of their respective masters. They conclude their own station in life is the better.

'Twas in that place of Scotland's isle,
That bears the name of Auld King Coil,          *Kyle, Ayrshire.*
Upon a sunny day in June,
When, wearing through the afternoon,
Two dogs who'd had to work since dine,
Forgathered once upon a time.

The first I'll name, they called him Caesar,
Was kept just for his honour's pleasure:
His hair, his size, his mouth, his lugs,          *Ears.*
Showed he was none of Scotland's dogs;
But he was whelped some place abroad,
Where sailors go to fish for cod.                  *Labrador.*

His lockéd, lettered new brass collar
Showed him the gentleman and scholar;
But though he was of high degree,
Upon his oath, no pride had he;
But liked to spend an hour in fun,
With a gipsy's cur he could outrun.
At church or market, mill or smithy,
No mongrel dog was e'er unworthy,
But he would be right glad to see him,
And roam the hills and byways with him.

The other was a ploughman's collie,
A rhyming, ranting, raving billie.
Whose master for a comrade had him,
And by some freak had Luath called him
After some dog in a Highland song,
Was made long since, Lord knows how long.

He was a friendly faithful tyke,
That ever jumped a ditch or dyke.
His honest, comely winsome face

Secured him friends in every place.
His breast was white, his shaggy back
Well-clad with coat of glossy black;
His bushy tail, with upward curl,
Hung o'er his hips with graceful swirl.

No doubt they were, fond of each other,
And thick as thieves with one another;
While both their noses sniffed away
At mice and moles among the hay.
They tired themselves with long excursions,
And vied each other in diversions;
Until with clowning weary grown,
Upon a knoll they sat them down,
And there began a long digression
About the lords of all creation.                    *Humans.*

## CAESAR

I've often wondered, honest Luath,
What sort of life poor dogs like you have;
For when of gentry's life I tell,
I thought all folks lived just as well.
My lord rakes in his rackéd rents,
His coals, his dues, and all his stents:        *Perquisites.*
He rises when he likes hisel',
His servants answer to the bell;
He calls his coach, he calls his horse,
He owns a heavy silken purse,
As long as my tail, where through the seam
The yellow golden guineas gleam.
From morn till night his cooks are toiling,
At baking, roasting, frying, boiling;
But when the gentry have their fill,
The servants too tuck in at will;
Our kennel lad, poor little sinner,
A woeful elf, he eats a dinner,
Better than any tenant man
His honour has in all his land.
But what poor cot folk fill their paunch with,
I own it's past my comprehension.

## LUATH

Truth Caesar, they have their trouble,
Digging away through mud and rubble,
With dirty stones building a dyke,
Baring a quarry and suchlike,
Himself, a wife, he thus sustains,
A couple of wee ragged bairns,
With nothing but his daily toil
To keep them all above the soil.
And when they meet with sore disasters,
Like loss of health, or want of masters,
You'd almost think, a wee touch longer
And they must starve of cold and hunger.
But how it is I've never kenned yet,
They're mostly wonderfully contented.
For stalwart men and clever lasses
Are bred in such a way as this is.


## CAESAR

But then to see how you're neglected,
How cursed and cuffed and disrespected;
Lord man, our gentry care as little
For diggers, ditchers and such cattle;
They raise their nose to those who labour
As they would to a stinking badger.
I've noticed on our lord's court day,
And many a time my hearts been wae,                     *Woeful.*
Poor tenant bodies, short of cash,
How they must bear the factor's gnash.
He'll stamp and threaten, curse and swear,
Apprehend them, impound their gear;
While they must stand with aspect humble,
And hear it all, and fear and tremble.
I see how folk live who have riches,
But surely poor folk must be wretches.

## LUATH

They're not so wretched as you would think,
Though constantly on poverty's brink;
They're so accustomed to the sight,
They view it all with little fright.
Then chance and fortune are so guided,
They are for more or less provided,
And though fatigued with hard employment,
The Day of Rest's a sweet enjoyment.          *Sundays.*
The dearest comfort of their lives,
Their thriving bairns and faithful wives,
The prattling things are just their pride,
That sweetens all their fireside,
And while twelvepennyworth of nappy          *Ale.*
Can make them all so gay and happy,
They lay aside their private cares
To mind their church and state affairs;
They'll talk of patronage and priests
With rising fury in their breasts,
Or talk of what taxation's coming,
And wonder at the folk in London.          *Government.*


As bleak-faced Hallowmass comes round,
You hear the jovial singing sound,
When rural life of every station,
Unite in common recreation;
Sly winks and wit, and social mirth,
Forgets there's Care upon the earth.


That merry day the year begins,
They bar the door on frosty winds;
The ale flows o'er in creaming foam,
Warming all hearts within the home;
The pipe and snuff are handed round;
Goodwill and cheer to all abound.
The old folks having a great carouse,
The young ones scampering through the house;
My heart has been so glad to see them,
That I for joy have barkéd with them.

Still it's true what you have said;
Great tragedies are often played;
There's many a credible stock
Of decent, honest, sore pressed folk
Are torn out by both root and branch,
Some rascal's prideful greed to quench,
Who seeks to ingratiate the faster,
In favour with some gentle master,
Who is away at Parliamenting,
For Britain's good his soul indenting.


## CAESAR

Forsooth my lad, you little know it,
For Britain's good? I'll always doubt it:
Say rather go as premiers lead him,
Say aye or no just as they bid him:
At operas and plays parading,
Mortgaging, gambling, masquerading;
Or maybe, as his tenants pay,
To Hague and Calais make his way,
To make the tour and take a whirl,
Learn the fashion, see the world.

There at Vienna or Versailles
He spends his father's old entails;                *Inheritance.*
And in Madrid abroad most nights,
He strums guitars, he sees bullfights;
Or down Italian vista startles,
Whore-hunting among the groves of myrtles:
Then sipping spa Germanic waters
To make himself look fair and fatter,
To clear the consequential sorrows,
Love gifts of carnival signoras.
For Britain's good? For her destruction,
With dissipation, feud, and faction.

## LUATH

Good gracious me, is that the way
They waste their fortunes while we may
Standing cowering and harassed,
And go along that way at last;
If they would stay away from courts,
Enjoy themselves with country sports,
It would for everyone be better,
The laird, the tenant and the cotter.
For they are frank, warm-hearted billies,
And none of them ill-mannered fellows;
Except for felling of their woodland,
And speaking slightenly of woman,
Or shooting of a hare or moor-cock,
They're not so bad or ill to poor folk.
But will you tell me, Master Caesar,
The great folk's life a life of pleasure?
The cold or hunger can ne'er come near them,
The thoughts of it need never fear them?


## CAESAR

Poor Luath, just suppose a change of places,
You'd never envy them their graces.
It's true they need not starve or sweat
Through winter's cold or summer's heat;
They've no hard work to craze their bones,
And fill old age with grips and groans;
But human beings are such fools,
For all their colleges and schools,
That when no real ills do perplex them,
They imagine just enough to vex them.

A country fellow at his plough,
His acres tilled by sweat of brow;
A country lassie at her wheel, *Spinning.*
Her dozens done, she feels so well.
Ladies and gents come off the worst,
When want of work their days are cursed.

They loiter, lounging, lank and lazy,
The Devil makes them feel uneasy;
Their days insipid, dull and tasteless;
And even their sports, their balls and races,
Their galloping through public places,
There's such parade, such pomp and art,
That joy can scarcely reach the heart.

The men wear out in sporting matches,
Then dabble away in deep debauches;
At night they're mad with drink and whoring,
Next day their life is past enduring.

The ladies arm in arm in clusters,
Are sweet and gracious, all as sisters;
But hear their thoughts of one that's absent,
No witch could utter thoughts so transcend.
While over their steaming cups of tea
Their slanderous tongues wag overfree.
Or through all night with weary looks,
Pore over the Devil's picture books;
Stake on a chance a farmer's stackyard,
And cheat like any unhung blackguard.
There's some exception, man and woman,
But this is gentry's life in common.

By now the sun was out of sight,
And darker gloaming brought the night.
The beetles flew with lazy drone;
The cows stood lowing in the lane;
When up they got and shook their lugs,
Rejoiced they were not men but dogs,
And each took off his several way,
Resolved to meet some other day.

## THE SELKIRK GRACE

Some have meat but cannot eat,
And some have none but want it.
We have meat and we can eat,
So let the Lord be thankéd

## MY HANDSOME NELL

This is the first composition of Burns; composed in his seventeenth year, it is left as it was written.

Oh once I loved a bonnie lass,
Ay, and I love her still,
And while that virtue warms my heart,
I'll love my handsome Nell.

As bonnie lasses I have seen,
And many full as braw,
But for the modest, gracfu' mien,
The like I never saw.

A bonnie lass I will confess,
Is pleasant to the e'e,
But without some better qualities,
She's no' a lass for me.

But Nellie's looks are blythe and sweet,
And, what is best of a',
Her reputation is complete,
And fair without a flaw.

She dresses aye so clean and neat,
Both decent and genteel,
And then there's something in her gait,
Gars any dress look weel.

A gaudy dress and gentle air,
May slightly touch the heart,
But it's innocence and modesty,
That polishes the dart.

'Tis this in Nellie pleases me,
'Tis this enchants my soul,
For absolutely in my breast,
She reigns without control.

## O FOR ONE AND TWENTY TAM

A young girl, with prospects, is impatient to attain twenty-
one years of age, and the independence it would bring.

I long for one and twenty
Come soon sweet one and twenty,
I'll show my kin just what I mean,
When I reach one and twenty.

They snub me sore, and hold me down,
And make me look so foolish,
But three short years will soon go by,
And then comes one and twenty.

A length of land, a little gold,
Was left me by my auntie,
With kith and kin I'll be more bold,
When I see one and twenty.

They'll have me wed some wealthy fool,
Though I myself have plenty,
But hear me well and hear my rule,
I'm Tam's at one and twenty.

## THE DUMFRIES VOLUNTEERS

Burns was a member of this military unit formed under the threat of a French invasion in 1795.

Does haughty Gaul invasion threat?
Then let the loons beware, sir;
There's wooden walls upon our seas,
And volunteers on shore, sir.
The Nith shall stop its seaward run,
And Criffel sink in Solway,                    *Mountain.*
Ere we permit a foreign foe,
On British soil to rally.

O let us not, like snarling tykes,             *Dogs*
In wrangling be divided;
Till, slap, in comes a foreign loon,
And with a gun decides it.
Be Britain still to Britain true,
Among ourselves united;
For never but by British hands
Must British wrongs be righted.

The union of the Church and State,
Perhaps will need some patching.
But never will a foreign rogue,
Ever knock a nail in't.
Our father's blood the Union bought,
And who would dare to spoil it,
By Heavens a sacrilegious dog,
Will never come to foil it.

The wretch who would a tyrant own,
And the wretch, his true-born brother,
Who's set the mob upon the throne,
May they be damned together
Who will not sing 'God save the King',
Shall hang as high's the steeple,
But while we sing 'God save the King',
We'll not forget the people.

## BESS AND HER SPINNING WHEEL

Sweet are the thoughts that savour of content.

I'm happy with my spinning wheel,
And happy with my wool to reel,
From head to toe it clothes me fine,
And wraps so softly me and mine.
I settle down to sing and spin,
While low descends the summer sun,
Blest with content, and milk and meal,
I'm happy with my spinning wheel.

On every hand the brooklets wend,
Up to my cottage by the bend,
The scented birch and hawthorne white
Across the pool their arms unite,
Alike to screen the birdie's nest,
And little fishes cooler rest:
The sun shines kindly where I dwell,
Where smoothly turns my spinning wheel.

On lofty oaks the pigeons croon,
And echo out their doleful tune;
The linnets in the bushes raise
Sweet songs that rival other lays.
The crakes among the clover run,
The partridge whirring in the sun,
The swallows swooping for their meal,
Amuse me at my spinning wheel.

With small to sell and less to buy,
Above distress, below envy,
Oh who would leave this humble state,
For all the pride of all the great,
Amid their flaring, idle toys,
Amid their cumbrous noisy joys?
Can they the peace and pleasure feel
Of Bessie at her spinning wheel?

# I'M FAR TOO YOUNG TO MARRY

I am my mother's only bairn,
With stranger folk I'm wary.
To lie in bed with a stranger man,
I'm afraid it would be eerie.

    I'm far too young, I'm far too young,
    I'm far too young to marry,
    I'm far too young, 'twould be a sin,
    To take me from my mammy.

My mam's bought me a brand new gown,
The church must have its gracing.
Were I to lie with you, kind sir,
I'm afraid you'd spoil the lacing.

Hallowmass has come and gone,
The nights are long in winter,
But you and I alone in bed,
In truth I dare not venture.

Full loud and shrill the frosty wind
Blows through the leafless timber,
But if you come this way again,
I'll older be by summer.

## MAN WAS MADE TO MOURN

This dirge reveals Burns in a sombre mood reflecting on a favourite theme, inequality, and contains several profound lines. For his subject he has chosen a poor blind great-uncle whom his mother knew and whose enjoyment was to cry while she sang to him 'The Life and Age of Man', the first verse of which ran:-

Upon the sixteen hunder year,
Of God and fifty three,
Frae Christ was born, that bought us dear,
As writings testifie;
On January the sixteenth day,
As I did lie alone,
With many a sigh and sob did say,
Ah, man is made to mourn.

When chill November's surly blast
Made fields and forests bare,
One evening, as I wandered forth
Along the banks of Ayr,
I spied a man, whose agéd step
Seemed weary, worn with care;
His face was furrowed o'er with years,
And hoary was his hair.

'Young stranger, wither wand'rest thou?'
Began the reverend sage;
'Does thirst of wealth thy step constrain,
Or youthful pleasures rage?
Or, haply, pressed with cares and woes,
Too soon thou hast began,
To wander forth, with me, to mourn,
The miseries of man.

'The sun that overhangs yon moors,
Out-spreading far and wide,
Where hundreds labour to support
A haughty lordling's pride:

I've seen yon weary winter sun
Twice forty times return;
And ev'ry time has added proofs
That man was made to mourn.

'O man, while in thy early years,
How prodigal of time,
Misspending all thy precious hours,
Thy glorious youthful prime,
Alternate follies take the sway;
Licentious passions burn;
Which tenfold force gives nature's law,
That man was made to mourn.

'Look not alone on youthful prime,
Or manhood's active might;
Man then is useful to his kind,
Supported is his right:
But see him on the edge of life,
With cares and sorrows worn,
Then age and want – oh ill-matched pair!
Show man was made to mourn.

'A few seem favourites of fate,
In fortune's lap caressed,
Yet, think not all the rich and great
Are likewise truly blest.
But, oh, what crowds in ev'ry land,
All wretched and forlorn;
Thro' weary life this lesson learn,
That man was made to mourn.

Many and sharp the numerous ills,
Inwoven with our frame,
More pointed still we make ourselves
Regret, remorse, and shame;
And man, whose heaven-erected face,
The smiles of love adorn,
Man's inhumanity to man
Makes countless thousands mourn.

See yonder poor o'erlaboured wight,
So abject, mean, and vile,
Who begs a brother of the earth
To give him leave to toil;
And see his lordly fellow worm
The poor petition spurn,
Unmindful, tho' a weeping wife
And helpless offspring mourn.

If I'm designed yon lordling's slave,
By nature's hand designed,
Why was an independent wish
Ever planted in my mind?
If not, why am I subject to
His cruelty and scorn?
Or why has man the will and power
To make his fellow mourn?

Yet, let not this too much, my son,
Disturb thy youthful breast:
This partial view of human-kind
Is surely not the last.
The poor, oppresséd, honest man,
Had never, sure, been born,
Had there not been some recompense
To comfort those who mourn.

O Death, the poor man's dearest friend,
The kindest and the best,
Welcome the hour my agéd limbs
Are laid with thee at rest.
The great, the wealthy, fear the blow,
From pomp and pleasure torn;
But, oh, a blest relief to those
That weary-laden mourn.'

## WHAT CAN A YOUNG LASSIE DO?

What can a young lassie, what shall a young lassie,
What can a young lassie do with an old man?
Bad luck on the money that tempted my mammy
To marry her Mary, for silver and land.

He's always complaining from morning till evening,
He spumes and he splutters the weary day long:
He's old and he's dozing, his blood it is frozen,
O, dreary's the night with a crazy old man.

He hums and he hankers, he frets and he cankers,
I never can please him, do all that I can:
He's peevish and jealous of all the young fellows:
O, woe on the day I wed an old man.

My old auntie Katie upon me takes pity,
I'll do my endeavour to follow her plan:
I'll cross him, I'll wreck him, until I heartbreak him,
And then his gold guineas will bring a young man.

## TO A MOUSE

Whilst ploughing on a November day Burns ruined the nest of a field mouse. He ponders why the creature runs away in such terror.


Oh, tiny timorous forlorn beast,
Oh why the panic in your breast?
You need not dart away in haste
    To some corn-rick.
I'd never run and chase thee,
    With murdering stick.

I'm truly sorry man's dominion
Has broken nature's social union,
And justifies that ill opinion
    Which makes thee startle
At me, thy poor earth-born companion,
    And fellow mortal.

I do not doubt you have to thieve;
What then? poor beastie you must live;
One ear of corn that's scarcely missed
    Is small enough:
I'll share with you all this year's grist,
    Without rebuff.

Thy wee bit housie too in ruin,
Its fragile walls the winds have strewn,
And you've nothing new to build a new one,
    Of grasses green;
And bleak December winds ensuing,
    Both cold and keen.

You saw the fields laid bare and waste,
And weary winter coming fast,
And cosy there beneath the blast,
    Thou thought to dwell,
Till crash: the cruel ploughman crushed
    Thy little cell.

Your wee bit heap of leaves and stubble,
Had cost thee many a weary nibble.
Now you're turned out for all thy trouble
     Of house and home,
To bear the winter's sleety drizzle,
     And hoar frost cold.

But, mousie, thou art not alane,
In proving foresight may be in vain,
The best laid schemes of mice and men,
     Go oft astray,
And leave us nought but grief and pain,
     To rend our day.

Still thou art blessed, compared with me!
The present only touches thee,
But, oh, I backward cast my eye
     On prospects drear,
And forward, though I cannot see,
     I guess and fear.

## THE DEATH AND DYING WORDS OF POOR MAILIE
### The author's pet ewe

As Mailie, and her lambs together,
Were one day nibbling on the tether,
Upon her hoof she caught a hitch,
And over she tumbled into a ditch:
There, groaning, dying, she did lie,
When simple Hughie ambled by.

With startled eye and lifted hands,
Poor Hughie like a statue stands;
He saw her days were near-hand ended,
But, woe's my heart, he could not mend it.
He gapéd wide, but nothing spoke,
At length Poor Mailie silence broke.

'O thou whose lamentable face
Appears to mourn my woeful case;
My dying words attentive hear,
And bear them to my master dear.

'Tell him, if ever again he keep,
Money enough to buy some sheep,
O, bid him never tie them up,
Be it lamb, or ewe, or randy tup.
But pasture them in park or hill,
And let them wander at their will;
So may his flocks increase to full,
To scores of lambs, with lots of wool.

'Tell him he was a master kind,
And always good to me and mine;
And now my dying charge I give him,
My helpless lambs, I trust them with him.

'O, bid him save their harmless lives,
From dog, and fox, and butchers' knives:
But give them good cow milk their fill,
Till they be fit to fend themselves.
And tend them duly, even and morn,
With tufts of hay and hands of corn.

'And may they never learn the manners,
Of other vile and low bred fellows,
That slink through hedge to eat and steal,
At stacks of peas, or stocks of meal.
So may they like their great forbears,
For many a year submit to shears;
So wives will give them bits of bread,
And bairns cry for them when they're dead.

My poor ram lamb, my son and heir,
I bid you bring him up with care,
And if he lives to be a beast,
To put some manners in his breast;
And warn him, what I will not name,
To stay content with ewes at hame;
And not to run and wear his hoofs,
Like other mean ungracious brutes.

And next my ewe lamb, silly thing,
God keep you from a tether string,
And may you never company keep
With any blasted moorland sheep;
But keep in mind, always forgather,
With rams of credit, like your father.

And now my bairns with my last breath,
I leave my blessings on you both,
And when you think upon your mother,
Mind to be kind to one another.

Now, honest Hughie, do not fail,
To tell my master all my tale,
And bid him burn this cursed tether,
And, for thy pains, you'll get my bladder.'      *In which to*
*boil haggis.*


This said, Poor Mailie turned her head,
And closed her eyes amongst the dead.

## POOR MAILIE'S ELEGY

Lament in rhyme, lament in prose,
With salt tears trickling down your nose,
Our poet's fate is at a close.
        Past all remead:
The last sad copestone of his woes;
        Poor Mailie's dead.


It's not the loss of worldly gear,
That could so bitter draw the tear,
Or make our poet, sadly wear
        The mourning weed;
He's lost a friend and neighbour dear,
        In Mailie dead.


Through all the town she trotted by him,
A long half mile she could descry him;
With kindly bleat when she did spy him;
        She ran with speed:
A friend more faithful ne'er came nigh him,
        Than Mailie dead.


She was a sheep with such good sense,
Her cultured manners were immense,
And never yet she broke a fence,
        Through thievish greed.
Our poet, lonely for all days hence,
        Now Mailie's dead.


Or, if he wanders lone and dreary,
Her living image in her yowie,            *Ewe lamb.*
Comes bleating to him in a hurry,
        For bits of bread;
The briny pearls gush in a flurry,
        For Mailie dead.

She was no scion of moorland tups,
With matted wool, and hairy hips;
For her forbears were brought in ships
    Let it be said:
No better sheep had yearly dips
    Than Mailie dead.

Rob cursed the man that first did render,
That vile unnatural thing, a tether,
Restricting lamb and sheep and wether
    With choking dread.
Never more they'll be together,
    For Mailie's dead.

O, all you bards on bonnie Doon,
And you in Ayr your chanters tune,
Come, join the melancholious croon
    O' Robin's reed,
His heart will never get aboon          *Above.*
    His Mailie dead.

# TO A HAGGIS

Haggis is a wholesome savoury pudding, a mixture of mutton and offal. It is boiled and presented at table in a sheep's stomach.

All hail your honest rounded face,
Great chieftan of the pudding race;
Above them all you take your place,
    Beef, tripe, or lamb:
You're worthy of a grace
    As long as my arm.

The groaning trencher there you fill,
Your sides are like a distant hill,
Your pin would help to mend a mill,        *Skewer*
    In time of need,
While through your pores the dews distil,
    Like amber bead.

His knife the rustic goodman wipes,
To cut you through with all his might,
Revealing your gushing entrails bright,
    Like any ditch;
And then, oh what a glorious sight,
    Warm, welcome, rich.

Then plate for plate they stretch and strive,
Devil take the hindmost, on they drive,
Till all the bloated stomachs by and by,
    Are tight as drums.
The rustic goodman with a sigh,
    His thanks he hums.

Let them that o'er his French ragout,
Or hotchpotch fit only for a sow,
Or fricassee that'll make you spew,
    And with no wonder;
Look down with sneering scornful view,
    On such a dinner.

Poor devil, see him eat his trash,
As feckless as a withered rush,
His spindly legs and good whip-lash,
    His little feet
Through floods or over fields to dash,
    O how unfit.

But, mark the rustic, haggis-fed;
The trembling earth resounds his tread,
Grasp in his ample hands a flail
    He'll make it whistle,
Stout legs and arms that never fail,
    Proud as the thistle.

You powers that make mankind your care,
And dish them out their bill of fare.
Old Scotland wants no stinking ware,
    That slops in dishes;
But if you grant her grateful prayer,
    Give her a haggis.

## THE SOLDIER'S RETURN

When wild war's deadly blast had blown,
And gentle peace returning,
With many a sweet babe fatherless,
And many a widow mourning,
I left the lines and tented fields,
Where long I'd been a lodger,
A humble knapsack all my wealth,
A poor but honest soldier.

A true light heart was in my breast,
My hand unstained by plunder,
And for fair Scotland once again,
I cheery on did wander.
I thought upon the river Coil,
I thought upon my Nancy,
I thought upon the witching smile,
That caught my youthful fancy.

At length I reached the bonny glen,
Where early life I'd sported,
I passed the mill and trysting thorn,
Where Nancy oft I'd courted;
Who spied I but my own dear maid,
Down by her mother's dwelling,
I turned around to hide the flood,
That in my eyes were swelling.

With altered voice quoth I, 'Sweet lass
Sweet as yon hawthorne blossom,
Oh happy happy may he be,
Who's dearest to thy bosom.
My purse is light, I've far to go,
And fain would be thy lodger,
I've served my King and Country, so
Take pity on a soldier.'

So wistfully she gazed on me,
And lovelier was than ever,
Quoth she, 'A soldier once I loved,

Forget him shall I never.
Our humble cot, our homely fare,
You freely shall partake of it,
That gallant badge, that dear cockade,
You're welcome for the sake of it.'

She gazed – she reddened like a rose,
Then, pale as any lily,
She sank within my arms and cried,
'Art thou my own dear Willie?'
'By him who made yon sun and sky,
By whom true love's regarded,
I am the man, and thus may still
True lovers be rewarded.

'The wars are over and I've come home,
And find thee still true-hearted;
Though poor in gear, we're rich in love,
And more, we'll ne'er be parted.'
Quoth she, 'My grandsire left me gold,
A farm that's furnished fairly,
And come my faithful soldier lad,
You're welcome to it dearly.'

For gold the merchants plough the main,
The farmer ploughs the manor,
But glory is the soldier's prize,
The soldier's wealth is honour.
The brave poor soldier ne'er despise him,
Nor count him as a stranger,
Remember he's his country's stay:
In day and hour of danger.

## THE BANKS OF DOON

This song tells of a tragic love affair (not one of the poet's). A respected young lady of rank had borne a child without the sanction of the Church; forsaken, she died of remorse.

Ye banks and braes of bonny Doon,　　　　　　　　*slopes*
How can ye bloom so fresh and fair,
How can ye chant, ye little birds,
While I'm so weary, full of care?
You'll break my heart thou warbling bird
That flitters through the flowering thorn,
You mind me of departed joys,
Departed – never to return.

You'll break my heart, thou bonny bird,
That sings beside thy mate,
For so I sat, and so I sang,
But knew not of my fate.
Oft did we roam by bonny Doon,
To see the rose and woodbine twine,
Where every bird sang of its love,
And fondly so did I of mine.

With lightsome heart I pulled a rose,
So sweet upon its thorny tree,
But my false lover stole my rose,
And ah! he left the thorn with me.
With lightsome heart I pulled a rose,
Upon a morn in June,
And so I flowered in the morn,
And so was ruined by noon.

## A RED RED ROSE

My love is like a red red rose,
That's newly sprung in June,
My love is like a melody
That's sweetly played in tune.

As fair thou art, my bonny lass,
So deep in love am I,
And I will love thee still, my dear,
Till all the seas run dry.

Till all the seas run dry, my dear,
And rocks melt with the sun,
I will love thee still, my dear,
While the sands of life shall run.

And fare you well, my only love,
And fare you well awhile,
And I will come again, my love,
Though it were ten thousand mile.

## ON THE POET'S DAUGHTER
(Who died in 1795)

Here lies a rose, a budding rose,
Blasted before its bloom,
Whose innocence did sweets disclose,
Beyond that flower's perfume.
To those who for her loss are grieved,
This consolation's given –
She's from a world of woe relieved,
And blooms, a rose, in heaven.

## THE HOLY FAIR

This satire by Burns is not, perhaps, on the Church itself, but upon its servants. It describes, with some levity, an out-door prayer, or revivalist meeting. There is the atmosphere of a modern Bank Holiday, with the crowd in relaxed gaiety.

Upon a summer Sunday morn,
When nature's face is fair,
I walkéd forth to view the corn,
And smell the clean fresh air.
The rising sun, o'er Galston moors,
With glorious light was shining,
The hares were jumping off all fours,
The skylarks they were singing,
  So sweet that day.

As lightsomely I looked abroad,
To see a scene so gay,
Three maidens, early on the road,
Came tripping up the way.
Two had mantles of mourning kind,
One with a gray cloth lining,
The third, who was a pace behind,
Was in the fashion shining,
  Full gay that day.

The two appeared like sisters twin,
In feature, form and clothes,
Their visage, withered, long and thin,
And sour as any sloes.
The third came up, hop step and jump,
As light as any fairy,
With curtsy low, she made a bow,
As soon as e're she saw me,
  Full kind that day.

With bonnet off quoth I, 'Sweet lass,
I think you seem to know me,
I'm sure I've seen your pretty face,
But yet I cannot name ye.'

Quoth she, and laughing as she spoke,
And takes me by the hands,
'You for my sake have given the most,
Of all the Ten Commands
          Full ear this day.

My name is Fun, your crony dear,
Your dearest friend you see,
And this is Superstition here,
And that's Hypocrisy.
I'm going to Mauchline Holy Fair,
To spend an hour in daffing,                    *Merriment.*
If we go there, with yon wrinkled pair,
We'll get some fits of laughing,
          At them this day.'

Quoth I, 'With all my heart I'll come with you,
And put my Sunday shirt on,
And meet you on the holy spot,
And now I'll get a spurt on.'
Then I went home at breakfast time,
And soon I made me ready,
For roads were full from side to side,
With many a merry body,
          In droves that day.

Here farmers trim in riding clothes,
Along with jogging cotters,
There smart young men without their woes,
Are springing o'er the gutters.
The lasses with their swaying rumps,
In silks and scarlets glitter,
With sweet milk cheese in gen'rous lumps,
And scones all spread with butter,
          To eat that day.

The collecting plate that's by the door,
Is heapéd up with ha'pence,
The surly sidesman gives a lour,
And makes us pay our twopence.
Then in we go to see the show,

On every side they're gath'rin,
Some carry planks, or chairs, or stools,
And some are busy blethering,
    Right loud that day.

Here stands a shed to fend the showers,
To screen our country gentry,
There's racer Jesse and two-three whores,
Are waiting at the entry;
Here sits a row of chatting maids,
With heaving breast and bare neck,
And there a batch of weaver lads,
Blackguarding from Kilmarnock,
    For fun that day.

Here some are thinking on their sins,
And some upon their clothes,
One curses feet that kicked his shins,
Another counts his woes.
On this hand sits a chosen batch,
With screwed-up sour faces,
On that a pair of chaps on watch,
To show girls to their places,
    On chairs that day.

O happy is the man and blest,
No wonder that it pride him,
Whose own dear lass whom he loves best
Comes sitting down beside him.
His hand at rest on her chair back,
He neatly does compose him,
Which, by degrees, slips round her neck,
And lands upon her bosom,
    Unseen that day.

Now all the congregation's kept
In silent expectation,
For Moody climbs the holy step,          *Pulpit.*
With tidings of damnation.
If the Devil, as in ancient days,

'Mong sons of god present him,
The very sight of Moody's face,
To his hot home would send him                    *Hell.*
        With fright that day.


Hear how he clears the points of faith,
With roaring and with thumping,
Now meekly calm, now wild in wrath,
Now stamping and now jumping.
His lengthened chin, his turned up snout,
His curdling squeals and gestures,
Oh how they fire the heart devout,
Like scalding mustard plasters
        On such a day.


But, hark, the pulpit's changed its tune,
There's peace and rest no longer;
The congregation all arise,
They cannot sit for anger.
Smith opens out his cold harangues,
On practice and on morals,
And out the godly go in throngs,
To give the jugs and barrels
        A lift that day.


What signifies his barren shine
Of moral powers and reason?
His English style and gesture fine
Are all clean out of season,
Like Socrates or Antonine,
Or some other pagan heathen.
The moral man he does define,
But ne'er a word of faith in
        That's right that day.


In good time comes an antidote,
Against such poisoned nostrum;
For Peebles, always the people's friend,
Ascends the holy rostrum:
See, up he's got the word of god

And meek and mild has viewed it.
While Commonsense has fled abroad,
And running through the open gate,
    Fast, fast, that day.

Wee Miller, next the guard relieves,
On orthodoxy rambles,
Though in his heart he well believes,
And thinks it's old wives fables.
But faith, his reverence wants a Manse,
So craftily he cons them;
Although his worldly wit and sense,
Does sometimes overcome him
    At times that day.

Now all the rooms the change house fills,
With drunken commentators;
They're crying out for bread and gills,
And make the pint pots clatter.
While thick they throng, and loud and long,
With logic and with scripture,
They raise a din that in the end,
Is like to breed a rupture
    Of wrath that day.

Give me my drink, it gives me more,
Than either school or college:
It kindles wit, it wakens lore,
It fills us full of knowledge.
If it's whisky raw, give us some more,
Or any stronger potions,
It never fails to cure your ills,
And sharpens all perceptions
    By night or day.

The lads and lasses blithely bent
To mind both soul and body,
Sit round the table, well content,
Stirring round their toddy.
On this one's dress, and this one's looks,

They're making observations,
While some are cosy in a nook,
And forming assignations
          To meet some day.

But now the Lord's own trumpet sounds,
Till all the hills are roaring,
And echoes back return the shouts:
Black Russel is not sparing.
His piercing words, like Highland swords,
Divide your bone and marrow;
His talk of hell, where devils dwell,
Our very soul does harrow
          With fright that day.

A vast, unbottomed, boundless pit,
Filled full with burning brimstone,
Whose raging flame and scorching heat,
Would melt the hardest whinstone.          *Granite.*
The half asleep start up with fear,
And think they hear it roaring,
When all the time it does appear,
It was some neighbour snoring
          Asleep that day.

'Twould be too long a tale to tell,
Of many stories past,
Of how they crowded to the bar
When they were all dismissed.
How drink went round in jugs and cups,
Among the chairs and benches,
And cheese and bread from women's laps,
Was dealt about in lunches
          For all that day.

In comes a plump and homely wife,
And sits down by the fire,
Displays her cheeses and her knife;
The lasses all are shyer.
The old goodmen about the place,

From side to side they stagger,
Till someone by his bonnet lays,
And gives them all a lecture.'
    Full long that day.

Alas for him who gets no lass,
Or lasses that get nothing,
Small need has he to say a grace,
Or spoil his brand new clothing.
O, wives be mindful, once yourself,
How many lads you wanted,
And do not for a piece of cheese,
Let lasses be affronted.'
    On such a day.

Now rings the bell with rattling line,
With joyful peal and croon;
Some swagger home all full and fine,
Some wait till afternoon.
At stiles the laddies halt awhile,
Where lasses cool their heels,
With faith and hope, and love they smile,
They trust their passion yields
    Some fruit that day.

How many hearts this day converts,
Of sinners and of lasses.
Their hearts of stone, by night have gone,
As soft as any flesh is.
There's some that's full of love divine,
There's some whose hearts will falter,
But some affairs that day began
Will end before the altar,
    Some future day.

## MY HEART WAS ONCE

My heart was once so blythe and free,
As summer days were long;
But a young and handsome weaver lad
Soon made me change my song.

> To the weavers never go, fair maids,
> To the weavers never go,
> I warn you right, go ne'er at night,
> To the weavers never go.

My mother sent me to the town,
To weave some tartan cloth,
But the long and weary weaving o't,
Had brought me sighs and wrath.

A young and handsome weaver lad,
Set working at his loom;
He took my heart as with a net,
When he glanced across the room.

I sat beside my warping wheel,
As it spun round and round,
At every weave and every warp,
My heart it gave a bound.

The moon was sinking in the west,
With visage pale and wan,
As my youthful handsome weaver lad,
Convoyed me through the glen.

But what was said, and what was done,
For shame I cannot tell,
But oh, I fear my folk quite soon,
Will know as well's mysel'.

## VERSES TO MY BED

Thou bed, in which I first began,
To be that various creature – man;
And when again the fates decree,
The place where I will cease to be;
When sickness comes, to whom I fly,
To soothe my pain, or close my eye;
When care surrounds me, where I weep,
Or lose them all in balmy sleep;
When sore with labour, whom I court,
And to thy downy breast resort;
Where, too, ecstatic joys I find,
When deigns my Delia to be kind,
And full of love, in all her charms,
Thou giv'st the fair one to my arms.
The centre thou, where grief and pain,
Disease and rest alternate reign.
Oh, since within thy little space
So many various scenes take place,
Lessons as useful shalt thou teach,
As sages dictate, churchmen preach;
And man, convinced by thee alone,
This great important truth shall own:-
That thin partitions do divide
The bounds where good and ill reside;
That nought is perfect here below,
But bliss still bord'ring upon woe.

## THE COTTER'S SATURDAY NIGHT
### Inscribed to Robert Aiken, Esq.

This, surely, must be the most sublime creation of Robert Burns. Modelled on his own family and written a year after his father's death, it has the same theme as Gray's *Elegy*, a verse of which is taken as the text.

> Let not ambition mock their useful toil,
> Their homely joys, and destiny obscure.
> Nor grandeur hear with a disdainful smile,
> The short but simple annals of the poor.
>
> GRAY.

My loved, my honoured, much respected friend,
No mercenary bard his homage pays;
With honest pride I scorn each selfish end;
My dearest meed, a friend's esteem and praise:
To you I sing in simple Scottish lays,
The lowly train in life's sequestered scene,
The native feelings strong, the guileless ways;
What Aiken in a cottage might have been;
Ah, though his worth unknown, far happier there I ween.

November chill blows loud with angry sough:
The short'ning winter day is near a close;
The miry beasts retreating from the plough;
The black'ning train of crows to their repose:
The toil-worn cotter from his labour goes,
This night his weekly toil is at an end,
Collects his spades, his mattocks, and his hoes,
Hoping the morn in ease and rest to spend,
And weary, o'er the moor, his course does homeward bend.

At length his lonely cot appears in view,
Beneath the shelter of an agéd tree;
The expectant wee things, toddling, stagger through
To meet their dad, with fluttering noise and glee.
His wee bit ingle, blinking bonnily,

His clean hearthstone, his thrifty wifie's smile,
The lisping infant prattling on his knee,
Does all his weary workday cares beguile,
And makes him quite forget his labour and his toil.

And soon the elder bairns come dropping in,
At service out, among the farmers' round;
Some tend the plough, some herd, or sometimes
Run an errand to a neighbour town.
Their eldest hope, their Jenny, woman grown,
In youthful bloom, love flushing both her cheeks
Comes home, perhaps to show her brand new gown,
Or render hard-won wages, for she seeks
To help her parents dear, if they in hardship be.

With joy unfeigned, brothers and sisters meet,
And each from each they calm their fears:
The social hours, swift-winged, unnoticed, fleet;
Each tells the other what he sees or hears;
The parents, partial, eye their hopeful years,
Anticipation points the view.
The mother with her needle and her shears,
Makes old clothes as good as new;
The father mixes all with admonition due.

Their master's and their mistress's commands,
The youngsters are warnéd to obey;
To tend their labours with a steady hand,
And ne'er, though out of sight, to joke or play:
And O, be sure to fear the Lord alway;
And mind your duty, duly, morn and night;
Lest in temptation's path you go astray,
Implore His counsel and assisting might:
They never sought in vain that sought the Lord aright.

But hark, a rap comes gently to the door;
Jenny, who knows the meaning of the same,
Tells how a neighbour lad came o'er the moor,
To do some errands and convoy her hame.
The wily mother sees the conscious flame

Sparkle in Jenny's eye, and flush her cheek:
With heart-struck anxious care enquires his name,
While Jenny is half afraid to speak;
Well-pleased the mother hears, he's not a worthless rake.


With kindly welcome Jenny brings him in;
A strapping youth; he takes the mother's eye;
Blythe Jenny sees his visit is no sin;
The father talks of horses, ploughs, and kye;     *Cattle.*
The youngster's artless heart o'er flows with joy,
The mother, with a woman's wiles, can spy
What makes the youth so bashful and so grave;
Well-pleased to think her girls respected like the lave.     *Rest.*


O happy love – where love like this is found,
O heart-felt rapture, bliss beyond compare;
I've pacéd much this weary mortal round,
And sage experience bids me this declare:–
'If Heaven a draught of heavenly pleasure spare,
One cordial in this melancholy vale,
'Tis when a youthful, loving, modest pair,
In other's arms breath out the tender tale,
Beneath the milk-white thorn that scents the evening gale.'


Is there, in human form, that bears a heart –
A wretch, a villain, lost to love and truth,
That can, with studied, sly, ensnaring art,
Betray sweet Jenny's unsuspecting youth?
Curse on his perjured arts, dissembling smooth.
Are honour, virtue, conscience, all exiled?
Is there no pity, no relenting ruth,
Points to the parents fondling o'er their child?
Then paints the ruined maid, and their distraction wild.


But now the supper crowns their simple board,
The wholesome porridge, chief of Scotland's food,
The milk their only cow can scarce afford,
That beyond the hallway chews the cud,
The dame brings forth in complimental mood,

To tempt the lad, her choicest cheese,
And oft he's pressed, and oft he calls it good;
The frugal wife, garrulous will tell
It is a twelvemonth old, since heather was in the bell.

The cheerful supper done, with serious face
They round the ingle form a circle wide;
The sire turns over with patriarchal grace
The family Bible, once his father's pride:
His bonnet reverently is laid aside,
His graying hair wearing thin and bare;
Those strains that once in Zion glide,
Intones a chapter with judicious care;
And 'let us worship God' he says, with solemn air.

They chant their artless notes in simple guise;
They tune their hearts, by far the noblest aim;
Perhaps Dundee's wild-warbling measures rise,
Or plaintive Martyrs, worthy of the name;
Or noble Elgin beats the heavenward flame,
The sweetest far of Scotland's holy lays:
Compared with these, Italian trills are tame;
The tickled ear no heartfelt raptures raise;
No unison have they with our creator's praise.

The priest-like father reads the sacred page,
How Abraham was the friend of God on high;
Or Moses bade eternal warfare wage
With Amalek's ungracious progeny;
Or how the royal bard did groaning lie
Beneath the stroke of Heaven's avenging fire;
Or Job's pathetic plaint, and wailing cry;
Or rapt Isaiah's wild, seraphic fire;
Or other holy seers that tune the sacred lyre.

Perhaps the Christian volume is the theme,
How guiltless blood for guilty man was shed;
How He, who bore in heaven the sacred name,
Had not on earth whereon to lay His head:
How His first followers and servants sped;

The precepts sage they wrote to many a land:
How He alone in Patmos banishéd,
Saw in the sun a mighty angel stand,
And heard great Bab'lon's doom pronounced by Heaven's
  command.

Then kneeling down, to Heaven's Eternal King,
The saint, the father, and the husband prays:
Hope 'springs exulting on triumphant wing',
That thus they all shall meet in future days:
There ever bask in uncreated rays,
No more to sigh, or shed the bitter tear,
Together hymning their creator's praise,
In such society, yet still more dear,
While circling time moves round in an eternal sphere.

Compared with this, how poor Religion's pride
In all the pomp of method, and of art,
When men display to congregations wide
Devotion's every grace, except the heart.
The Power, incensed, the pageant will desert,
The pompous strain, the sacerdotal stole;
But haply, in some cottage far apart,
May hear, well-pleased, the language of the soul;
And in his book of life the inmates poor enrol.

Then homeward each take off their several way;
The younger cottagers retire to rest;
The parent-pair their secret homage pay,
And proffer up to heaven the warm request
That He who stills the raven's clamorous nest,
And decks the lily fair in flowery pride,
Would, in the way His wisdom sees the best,
For them and for their little ones provide;
But, chiefly, in their hearts with grace divine preside.

From scenes like this old Scotland's grandeur springs,
That make her loved at home, revered abroad:
Princes and lords are but the breath of kings,
'An honest man's the noblest work of God,'
And Certes, in fair virtue's heavenly road,

The cottage leaves, the palace far behind;
What is a lordling's pomp? – a cumbrous load,
Disguising oft the wretch of humankind,
Studied in the arts of hell, in wickedness refined.

O Scotland, my dear, my native soil,
For whom my warmest wish to heaven is sent;
Long may your hardy sons of rustic toil,
Be blest with health, and peace, and sweet content.
And, O may Heaven their simple lives prevent
From luxury's contagion, weak and vile;
Then, however crown and coronets be rent,
A virtuous populace may rise the while,
And stand a wall of fire around their much-loved isle.

O Thou, who poured the patriotic tide
That streamed through Wallace's undaunted heart;
Who dared to nobly stem tyrannic pride,
Or nobly die, the second glorious part,
(The patriot's God peculiarly Thou art,
His friend, inspirer, guardian, and reward),
O never, never Scotland's realm desert:
But still the patriot, and the patriot bard,
In bright succession raise, her ornament and guard.

## WILLIE'S WIFE

Willie Wastle dwelt on Tweed,
The spot they call it Linkum-doddie,
Willie was a weaver good,
Could weave a cloth with anybody.
He had a wife both dour and dim,
Old gypsy Meggie was her mother;
Such a wife as Willie had,
I would not give a button for her.

She has an eye – she has but one,
The cat has two the very colour,
Four rusty teeth, forbye a stump,
A voice to deafen the dusty miller.
A whispy beard about her mouth,
A nose and chin that come together,
Such a wife as Willie had,
I would not give a button for her.

Her legs are bowed, with ankles thin,
One limping leg a hand breadth shorter;
She's twisted right, she's twisted left,
To balance fair in every quarter.
She has a hump upon her chest,
The twin of that upon her shoulder.
Such a wife as Willie has,
I would not give a button for her.

Old tabby by the fire sits,
With her paw her face awashing;
But Willie's wife is not so clean,
She wipes her face upon a cushion.
Her ample fists like fisher's creels,
Her face would foul Sweet Afton Water.
Such a wife as Willie had,
I would not give a button for her.

# THE GUIDWIFE OF WAUCHOPE HOUSE TO ROBERT BURNS

The goodwife, Mrs Scott, a painter and poetess, admired the poems of Burns, but doubted that he could really be a ploughman. Here is her poem to Burns ('translated'), followed by his reply.

My merry, witty, rhyming ploughman,
I have my doubts it is not true man,
That you behind the plough were bred,
With ploughmen schooled, and ploughmen fed,
I doubt it sore, you've drawn your knowledge,
From grammar school or college.

Good truth, your soul and body both
Were better fed, I'll give my oath,
Than theirs, who sup sour milk and porridge,
And through The Holy Bible forage.

Whoever heard a ploughman speak,
And tell if Homer was a Greek,
He'd flee as soon upon a cudgel,
As give a single line of Virgil.

And then so sly you make your jokes,
Of Willie Pitt and Charlie Fox,                    *Statesmen.*
Our greatest men you well describe,
On how to make the nation thrive,
I'd almost swear you dwelt among them,
And as you saw them, so you sung them.

But be ye ploughman be ye peer,
A funny blade you are, I swear,
And though the cold I ill can bide,
Yet twenty miles or more I'd ride,
O'er moss and moor and never grumble,
Though my old nag should give a stumble:
To chat a winter night with thee,
And hear your songs an sonnets slee.               *Sly.*

A good salt herring and a cake,
With such a man, a feast would make;
I'd rather drink your creaming ale,
And eat your bread and cheese and kale,
Than with dull lords on turtle dine,
And wonder at their wit and wine.

And if I knew just where you lived,
I'd send to you a tartan plaid;
'Twould keep your shoulders warm and dry,
Whene'er to church or mart you hie;
For south as well as north my lad,
A prudent Scot is warmly clad.
Though we are far from one another,
Yet proud I am to call thee brother.

In reply Burns sent her this poem, which shows that he had not forgotten his Handsome Nell of thirteen years ago.

## TO MRS. SCOTT OF WAUCHOPE

Guidwife:-
I mind it well, in early date,
When I was young with unknown fate,
And first could thresh the barn;
And hold the horses to the plough,
Exhausting work both then and now,
Yet very keen to learn;
When first among the yellow corn,
When manhood came to pass,
And with the rest each merry morn,
Attended with my lass                    *Handsome Nell.*
Then cutting and clearing
The newly stackéd row,
With laughing and daffin,                    *Fun.*
We wore the day away.

Even then a wish, I mind its power –
A wish that to my latest hour
Shall strongly heave my breast,
That I for poor old Scotland's sake
Some useful plan or book to make,
Or sing a song at least.
The rough Burr-thistle, spreading wide    *National Emblem.*
Amidst the fields of growing corn,
The weeding shears I turned aside,
Lest our symbol I should mourn;
No nation, no station,
My envy e'er could raise;
A Scot still, but blot still,
I knew no higher praise.

But still the elements of song
In formless jumble, right or wrong,
Wild floated in my brain:
That harvest time I said before,
My partner in the merry corps,

She roused the forming strain:
I see her yet, the lovely quean,
That lighted up my jingle,
Her witching smile, her youthful mien
That made my heart strings tingle;
I was fired and inspired,
At every kindling keek,                          *Peep.*
But bashful, and fearful,
Was half afraid to speak.

Health to the sex, each fine fellow says
With merry dance in winter-days,
Have we to share in common:
The gust of joy, the balm of woe,
The soul of life, the heaven below,
In rapture-giving women.
You surly bums that hate the name,
Be mindful of your mother:
She, honest woman, may think shame
That you're connected with her.
You're mean men, you're no men,
Who slight the lovely dears;
To shame you, disclaim you,
An honest he-man swears.

For you not bred to barn or byre,
Who sweetly tunes the Scottish lyre,
I thank you for your line.
The tartan plaid you kindly spare,
I'd be grateful this to wear;
It would enhance me fine.
I'd be more proud to wear that wrap,
More prouder than the purple,          *Ceremonial-cloaks.*
Or any ermine from a trap,
Or any such-like bauble.
Farewell then, good health then,
And plenty for you all;
May losses and sorrows,
Ne'er at your doorway call.

## TO A LOUSE

On seeing one on a lady's bonnet in church. The last verse contains what is perhaps the most universal quotation from all of the works of Robert Burns.


Where are you going you crawling creeper?
Your impudence protects your future:
I will say this, you strut right fairly,
  Over gauze and lace;
Though faith, I fear you dine but sparely
  On such a place.

You ugly creeping filthy wonder,
Detested, shunned by saint and sinner,
How dare you set your feet upon her,
  So fine a lady:
Go somewhere else and seek your dinner
  On some poor body.

Away to some beggars' filthy mantle;
There you may creep, and crawl, and settle,
With other kindred jumping cattle,
  In shoals and nations,
Where finest combs can ne'er unsettle
  Your thick plantations.

Now hold you there, you're out of sight,
Behind the ribbons, snug and tight;
You're climbing high, you'll not be right
  Till you've got on it,
The very topmost, towering height
  Of madam's bonnet.

What insolence to poke your nose out,
As bold and brash as you dare flout.
Oh that I had some poisonous potion
  About me private,
I'd give you such a hearty portion,
  You'd ne'er survive it.

I wouldn't have been surprised to see
You strutting on the likes of me;
Or maybe on some scruffy boy's
     Old flannel shirt;
But madam's Sunday headpiece; fie,
     How dare you do it.

O madam, do not toss your head,
And spread the little beasts abroad:
You little know what lightning speed
     The varment's making;
Your twitchy finger ends I fear,
     Draws our attention.

Lord would you the power give us
To see ourselves as others see us:
It would from many a blunder free us
     From foolish notions:
What airs and graces would depart us
     And even devotions.

# O GOOD ALE COMES

Good ale comes and good ale goes;
Good ale makes me sell my hose,
Sell my hose and pawn my clothes.
Good ale keeps away my woes.

I had six oxen to the plough,
Sturdy creatures I'll avow;
I sold them all just one by one
For ale. Alas, they're all now gone.

Good ale keeps me lank and lazy,
Makes me flirt with servant hussie,
Sit on the stool and feel so low,                    +
Good ale keeps me in its throe.

+    The stool of repentance, that embarrassing piece of
church furniture upon which transgressors were required to
sit.

## TO JOHN KENNEDY

Mr Kennedy had expressed an interest in Burns' poems, in appreciation of which Burns sent him this invitation.

Now, Kennedy, if foot or horse,
Ever bring you in by Mauchline cross,
(Lord, man, there's lasses that would force
    A hermit's fancy;
And down the road in faith they're worse,
    None more so randy,).

But, as I'm saying, please step to Dow's,
And taste the ale their Johnnie brews,
Till some bit laddie brings me news
    That you are there;
And then we'll have a quiet booze,
    Without a care.

It's not like me to sit and swallow,
Then like a swine to puke and wallow;
But give me just a true good fellow
    With manners fine.
We'll drink enough to make us mellow,
    And then we'll shine.

Now if you rate all other folk
By the nature of their cloak,
And mock their poverty as a joke
    With bitter sneer,
With you no friendship will I brook,
    Nor yet come near.

But if, as I'm informéd well,
You hate all evil where e'er it dwell,
And flinty hearts that cannot feel –
    Come, sir, you're one of few,
And here's my hand to wish you well,
    And God be with you.

Mossgiel, 3d March, 1786.              Robert Burness.

# THE LASS WHO MADE THE BED FOR ME

When winter's wind was blowing cold,
As to the north I took my way,
The mirksome night did me enfold;
I knew not where to lodge till day.

A charming girl I chanced to meet
Just in the middle of my care,
And kindly she did me invite,
To walk into a chamber fair.

I bowed full low unto this maid,
And thanked her for her courtesy.
I bowed full low unto this maid,
And bade her make a bed for me.

She made the bed both large and wide,
With two white hands the sheets unrolled.
Her twinkling eyes betrayed a prize,
That was for me if I be bold.

She snatched the candle in her hand,
And from the chamber quickly sped.
I quickly called her back and said,
'Another pillow 'neath my head'.

This she laid below my head,
And servéd me with due respect,
And to salute her with a kiss,
I put my arms around her neck.

'Hold off your hands, young man,' she says,
'And do not so uncivil be;
If you have any love for me,
Respect a girl's virginity.'

Her hair was like the links of gold,
Her teeth were like the ivory,
Her cheeks like lilies dipped in wine,
The lass who made the bed for me.

Her bosom was the drifted snow,
Two drifted heaps so fair to see;
Her limbs like polished marble stone,
The lass that made the bed for me.

I kissed her over and over again,
And she knew not just what to say,
But lay between the holland sheets,
And said no more till break of day.

Upon the morrow when we rose,
I thanked her for her courtesy.
She only blushed and gave a sigh.
'Alas,' she said, 'you've ruined me.'

I clasped her waist and soothed her sighs,
For tears were twinkling in her eyes,
I said, 'My lassie, do not cry,
You'll always make the bed for me.'

## TO A KISS

Humid seal of soft affection,
Tenderest pledge of future bliss,
Dearest tie of young connections,
Love's first snowdrop, virgin kiss.

Speaking silence, dumb confession,
Passion's birth, and infant's play,
Dove-like fondness, chaste concession,
Glowing dawn of brighter day.

Sorrowing joy, adieu's last action,
When lingering lips no more must join.
What words can ever speak affection
So thrilling and sincere as thine?

## WHISTLE, AND I'LL COME TO YOU MY LAD

O warily step when you come to court me,
And come not unless the back door's ajar,
Then up the back lane let nobody see,
For mother and father they'll both be awa',

    O, whistle and I'll come to you my lad,
    O, whistle and I'll come to you my lad,
    Though father and mother should both go mad,
    O, whistle and I'll come to you my lad.

At church or at market when e'er you see me,
Pass by as though you cared not a flea,
But give me a wink of your bonny black e'e,
Yet look as you were not looking at me.

I'll vow and protest that you care not for me,
Although it's in secret my beauty you'll see,
But court not another, though joking you be,
For fear that she'll steal my fancy from me.

## TO A MOUNTAIN DAISY

This is another pastoral poem in the same vein as 'The Mouse'. Burns had uprooted a clump of daisies whilst ploughing. He elevates this most humble of flowers, at the same time illustrating his own reflective mood.

Wee, modest, crimson tippéd flower,
Thou's met me in an evil hour,
For I must crush among the stoure                    *Dust.*
    Thy slender stem;
To spare thee now is past my power,
    Thou bonnie gem.

Alas, it's not thy neighbour sweet,
The bonnie lark, companion meet,
Bending thee 'mong dewy wheat,
    With speckled breast,
When upward-springing, blythe to greet,
    The purpling east.

Cold blew the bitter-biting north
Upon thy early, humble birth,
Yet cheerfully you flowered forth
    Amid the storm,
Scarce raised above the parent earth
    Thy slender form.

The flaunting flowers our gardens yield,
High shelt'ring woods and walls their shield;
But thou, out in the open weald
    'Neath clod or stone,
Adorn the sere and stubbled field,
    Unseen, alone.

There, in thy scanty mantle clad,
Thy snow-white bosom sun-ward spread,
Thou lifts thy unassuming head
    In humble guise;
But now the plough uptears thy bed
    And low thou lies.

Such is the fate of artless maid,
Sweet flow'ret of the rural shade,
By love's simplicity betrayed
    And guileless trust,
Till she, like thee, all soiled is laid
    Low in the dust.

Such is the fate of simple bard,
On life's rough ocean luckless starr'd,
Unskilful he to note the card
    Of prudent lore,
Till billows rage, and gales blow hard,
    And whelm him o'er.

Such fate to suffering worth is given,
Who long with wants and woes has striven,
By human pride or cunning driven
    To misery's brink,
Till wrenched of every stay but Heaven,
    He, ruined, sink.

Even thou who mourns the daisies' fate,
That fate is thine – no distant date;
Stern Ruin's ploughshare drives elate,
    Full on thy bloom,
Till crushed beneath the furrow's weight,
    Shall be thy doom.

## HALLOWEEN

This festival is held on the night of 31st of October, when spirits, good and evil, are abroad. Scottish country folk used the occasion to forgather and pry into the future. Burns describes nine ways whereby a future spouse will be manifest.

> Yes, let the rich deride, the proud disdain,
> The simple pleasures of the lowly train;
> To me more dear, congenial to the heart,
> Our native charm, than all the gloss of art.
> Goldsmith.

Upon that night when fairies light
On hills and downlands dance,
All through the night, a splendid sight,
On sprightly palfries prance;
And Mab the Queen abroad is seen,
Beneath the pale moonlight,
There, up the cave, above the wave,
Among the rocks and streams
    They sport that night.

Among the bonnie winding banks,
Where Doon runs whimpling clear,
Where Bruce once ruled the martial ranks,
And shook his Carrick spear,
Some merry friendly country folks
Together did convene
To roast their nuts, and pool their stocks,
And hold their Halloween
    Full blythe that night.

The lasses fair, beyond compare,
Wear dresses that are fine;
Their faces glow, full sweetly show
Hearts loyal, warm, and kind:
The lads so smart, with lover's knots,
Well-knotted on their garter;
Some are shy, while some are bold,
Makes lasses' hearts beat faster
    With joy that night.

During darkness cabbages are pulled up by their roots. Their size, shape and form are an indication of their future spouse, whose sweetness or otherwise is determined by the taste of the pith.

Then first and foremost through the fields
The plants must be uprooted;
They close their eyes to see what yields,
And to whom they'll most be suited.
Poor simple Will fell off the cart,
And wandered through the cabbage,
For he had pulled, for his own part,
A stump fit for a savage,
　　　　So bent that night.

Then straight or crooked, soiled or clean,
They roar and hail each other;
The very wee things, toddling, run
With stumps across their shoulders,
And if the pith be sweet or sour,
With pocket knives they taste them;
Then snugly o'er a doorway
With gentle care they place them
　　　　To lie that night.

Should a maiden wish to ascertain if she will retain that status till marriage, then she should run a stalk of corn through her fingers. If the topmost ear remains then she will retain that state.

The lasses slip outside,
To pull their stalks of corn,
Then Rab slips out, and fools about
Behind the hedge of thorn:
He held poor Nelly hard and fast,
Her screeches brought the lasses;
For her modesty was almost lost,
Among the hay and grasses
　　　　With Rab that night.

A boy and a girl may, at the onset of reciprocated love,
determine on its permanency. Each place a nut side by side
in the fire and observe if they roast quietly together or jump
apart.

The thrifty housewife's hoarded nuts,
Are round and round divided,
And many lad's and lass's fates
Are there that night decided:
Some settle, searing, side by side,
And roast together trimly;
Some ease away with saucy pride,
And jump right up the chimney
        Full high that night.

Jean slips in two, with heedful eye;
Who they were, she would not tell;
But this one's Jock, and this one's me,
She says unto hersel':
He swooned o'er her, and she o'er him,
As though they'd never part;
Till woof: Jock's jumped away with vim,
And Jean? She had a broken heart
        That very night.

Poor Willie with his cabbage stump
Is paired with prudish Mary,
And Mary then began to pout,
To be coupled up with Willie:
Mary's nut gave such a jump
It landed on her stocking;
While Willie's leapt and sparked about,
In just the way he wanted
        To be that night.

Nell has the strawbed on her mind,
With her and Rab upon it,
In loving flame they place their nuts,
And make their wishes on it:
Nell's heart was dancing at the view,

She whispered Rab to stop it;
Rab's stolen kiss they'll never rue,
They plight their troth upon it,
  Unseen that night.

 Should a girl secretly, and at night, throw a strand of wool
across a kiln, the other end will be grasped by her intended.

Now Marian behind their backs,
Has thoughts on Andrew Bell;
She leaves the others at their cracks,    *Chatting.*
And slips out by hersel':
Then through the yard by devious tracks
Up to the kiln she goes,
Trying to find what she most lacks,
And over the kiln throws
  Her strand of wool that night.

She came back winded, full of sweat,
At that there was no joking,
For someone held the other end;
Good Lord but she was quaking:
But whether it was the devil himsel',
Or whether some other creature,
Or whether it was Andrew Bell,
She did not stop to venture
  To spy that night.

 Again, should a girl wish to know who will espouse her, she
should eat an apple, by candlelight, before a mirror, when
his likeness will appear.

Wee Jennie to her grannie says,
'Will you go with me, grannie?
I'll eat the apple at the glass
I got from uncle Johnnie:'
She puffed her pipe with all she'd got,
In wrath she was so vap'ring,
She noticed not, an ember hot,
Had spoiled her worsted apron
  With holes that night.

'You little hussie, brazen face,
How dare you try such sporting,
To ask the mirror on the wall,
To spell you out your fortune?
No doubt that you may get a sight,
Great cause you have to fear it,
For many a lass has got a fright,
And should never have gone near it
    On such a night.'

---

The harvest before the Sheriffmuir,        *1715.*
I mind it as well as yestreen,
I was a wayward girl I'm sure,
I was'nt past fifteen;
The summer had been cold and wet,
The harvest poor and green,
But still a jovial time we had,
And kept our Halloween
    As it fell that night.

---

    If, sometime between dusk and dawn, a man should sow some hempseed, he will, upon looking behind him, discern the form of his future wife.

Our leading man was Rab M'Graen,
A clever sturdy fellow;
His son got Mary Sims with child,
Who lived in Achmacalla:
He got hempseed, I mind it well,
But maintained it was no matter,
Was churlish and beside himsel',
And angry at the banter
    That very night.

Then up got fighting Jamie Fleck,
And he swore by his conscience
That he'd sow hempseed a peck,        *¼ Bushel.*
And prove it all nonsense.
The old goodman got down his poke,

And out a handful gave him,
Then bade him slip from 'mong the folk
Sometime when none could see him
        And try it that night.


He marches out among the stacks,
Though he was somewhat frightened;
A fork he for a harrow takes,
And drags it o'er the stackyard,
And every now and then he says,
'Hemp seed I sow thee,
And her that is to be my lass,
Come after me and show me.'
        This very night.


He whistled up Lord Lennox's march,
To keep his courage cheerie,
Although his hair began to arch;
He was afraid and eerie.
Till presently he hears a squeak,
And then a groan and grunt,
And o'er his shoulder takes a peep,
Lest it was a little runt
        After him that night.


He screamed a horrid murder shout,
In dreadful desperation.
And young and old came running out,
To hear his wild narration.
He swore it was old Jean M'Craw,
Or crooked Marion Humphrey,
Then all stood back and gave a roar,
When all beheld the old stud boar
        Abroad that night.


Once more a maiden's task; she must go to a barn, alone
and at midnight, and go through the motions of winnowing.
The apparition that then appears will be that of her future
husband.

Meg fain would to the barn have gone,
To winnow piles of nothing,
But for to meet the Devil alone,
She had no stomach for it.
She bribes a lad with pickle nuts,
And two red-rosy apples,
To watch, while to the barn she goes,
In hopes to see Tam Kipples
      That very night.

She turns the key so carefully,
And o'er the threshold ventures;
Next to the lad she gives a call,
Then boldly in she enters.
A rat then scampered up the wall,
She cried, 'Good Lord preserve me,'
As in the dung pit she did fall,
She prayed with zeal and fervour
      Full fast that night.


If a man walks three times round a beanstack, the first
object that he enfolds is indicative of his future wife.

They urged out Will with sage advice,
They promised him a darling;
It chanced the stack he'd walked round thrice,
Was timber-propped 'gainst leaning.
Mistakes a knotted old moss-oak,
For some black gruesome carlin,        *Old woman.*
He swore an oath, near had a stroke,
His skin in shreds went peeling
      Off him that night.


A woman should dip her left sleeve in a south-running
stream at a point where three properties converge. Upon
drying the sleeve she will perceive, within the steam arising
therefrom, the object of her imaginations. The veracity of
this manifestation is confirmed in the penultimate verse of
'Tam Glen'.

A wanton widow Lizzie was,
As cheerful as a kitten,
But in the woods she had good cause,
To be severely bitten.
She through the whins, and by the cairn,
And o'er the hills she flitted;
Where three lairds' lands met at a burn,                    *Stream.*
To dip her shirt sleeve in it
      She went that night.

While o'er a rock the water plays,
As through the glen it whimpled,
While round a rocky bend it strays,
While in an eddy dimpled;
While glittering in the nightly rays,
With bickering, dancing dazzle;
While flowing neath the heathered braes,                    *Banks.*
Below the speading hazel,
      Unseen that night.

Among the bracken on the brow,
Between her and the moon,
The Devil, or else a straying cow,
Gave out an eerie croon:
Poor Lizzie's heart it had a turn,
Near skylark height went jumping;
She missed her step and in the burn,
Head over heels went bumping
      With a plunge that night.

    Blindfolded, one has the chance of putting a hand into one of three bowls. The one of clean water promises married bliss, the one of dirty water marital discord, while the empty third betokens a life of celibacy.

In rank upon the clean hearthstone,
Three dishes are arranged,
And every time, to fool no-one,
They're duly re-arranged:
Old uncle John, who wedlock joys,

For long years did desire
But always picked the empty dish,
Then threw them on the fire
    In wrath that night.

---

With merry songs and friendly chat,
Of these they did not weary;
With eerie tales and joyful jokes,
Their fun was cheap and cheerie;
Till buttered scones, with fragrant smells,
Set all their mouths a-watering,
Then with a social glass of ale,
They went their way careering
    Full blythe that night.

---

## THERE'LL NEVER BE PEACE
## TILL JAMIE COMES HAME

James II of England, who was also James VII of Scotland, was obliged to quit Britain in 1688.

By yon castle wall, at the close of the day,
I heard a man singing, though his head it was grey,
And as he was singing, the tears fast down came.
There'll never be peace till Jamie comes hame.

The Church is in ruins, the State likens Mars,
Delusions, oppressions, and murderous wars;
We dare not well say it, though we know who's to blame.
There'll never be peace till Jamie comes hame.

My seven fine sons for Jamie drew sword,
And now their green mounds are in the churchyard.
It broke the sweet heart of my faithful old dame.
There'll never be peace till Jamie comes hame.

Now life is a burden that bows me down,
Since I lost my sons and he lost his crown.
But till my last moments my words are the same:
There'll never be peace till Jamie comes hame.

## THE AMERICAN WAR

The first four verses are surely the briefest history of this war. The remaining five verses deal with the political intrigues in Britain in its aftermath.

| | |
|---|---|
| When Guilford good our pilot stood, | *Brit. statesman.* |
| And did our helm turn, man, | |
| One night at tea, began a plea, | |
| Within America, man: | |
| Then up they got, tea-chests the lot, | |
| And in the sea did throw them, | |
| And did no less, in full congress, | |
| Than quite refuse our law, man. | |

| | |
|---|---|
| Then through the lakes Montgomery takes, | *American General.* |
| He wasn't slow at all, man, | |
| Down Lowries burn he took a turn, | *St. Lawrence.* |
| And Carleton backed away, man: | *Brit. commander.* |
| But nevertheless, he at Quebec, | |
| Montgomery-like did fall, man, | *Killed.* |
| With sword in hand, before his band, | |
| Among his enemies all, man. | |

| | |
|---|---|
| Poor Tammy Gage, within a cage | *Brit. General.* |
| Was trapped at Boston Hall, man; | |
| Till Willie How, then showed them how | *Brit. General.* |
| The way to Philadelphia. | |
| With sword and gun he thought a sin, | |
| Good Christian blood to draw, man; | |
| But at New York, some bloody work | |
| He wrecked upon their cattle. | |

| | |
|---|---|
| Burgoyne went up, like spur and whip, | *Brit. General.* |
| Till Fraser brave did fall, man; | |
| Then lost his way, one misty day, | |
| In Saratoga shaw, man. | *Wood.* |
| Cornwallis fought without a doubt; | *Brit. Lord.* |
| He did the Yankees claw, man, | |
| But Clinton's sword from rust to save, | *Brit. General.* |
| He hung it on the wall, man. | *Surrendered.* |

Then Montague, and Guilford too,
Began to fear a fall, man,
And Sackville pure, withstood the lure,
The German chief to thwart man:        *King George III.*
Poor Paddy Burke, like any Turk,
No mercy had at all, man;
And Charlie Fox stood by his box,
And ranted at them all, man.


Then Rockingham took up the game,
Till death did on him call, man;
When Shellbourne weak held up his cheek,
Conform to gospel law, man;
St. Stephen's boys, with jarring noise.        *Parliament.*
They did his measures block, man;
For North and Fox united stocks,
And bore him to the wall, man.


Then clubs and hearts were Charlie's cards;
He swept the stakes away, man,
Till the diamond ace, of India race,
Made more mistakes to mend, man:
The English lads, with loud hurrahs,
On Chatham's boys did call, man,
And Scotland drew her pipes and blew,
'Up, Willie, beat them all, man.'


Behind the throne then Grenville's gone,
A secret word or two, man;
While sly Dundas aroused the class        *Scotsmen.*
Above the Roman Wall, man:
And Chatham's ghost, in heavenly cloth,
(Inspiréd bardies saw, man)
With kindling eyes cried, 'Willie rise,
Would I have feared them all, man'?

But, word and blow, North, Fox, and Co.,
Knocked Willie like a ball, man,
Till the English rose, cast off their clothes
Behind him in a row, man;
And Scotland then threw by the drone,
And did her knife draw out, man;
And swore full rude, through dirt and blood,
To make it good in law, man.

## LINES ON
## RETURNING A NEWSPAPER TO THE LENDER

These lines sustain the maxim that 'there is nothing new under the sun'. With just a little transposing it would be topical.


Kind Sir, I've read your paper through,
And, faith, to me 'twas really new.
How guessed you, sir, what most I wanted?
This many a day I've groaned and grunted
To know what French mischief was brewing;
Or what the devious Dutch were doing;
That vile back-slapper, Emperor Joseph,
If Venus yet has got his nose off;
Or how the eternal quarrel works,
Between the Russians and the Turks;
Or if the Swede, before he halts.
Would play another Charles the Twelfth:
Of Denmark, if you should know it;
Or Poland, and now who owns it?
How cut-throat Prussian blades were swinging,
How divided Italy was singing;
If Spaniards, Portuguese, or Swiss,
Were saying or taking ought amiss:
Or how our merry lads at hame
In Britain's court kept up the game;
How royal George, the Lord look o'er him;
Was managing St. Stephen's forum;     *Parliament.*
If sneaky Chatham Will was living;
Has thoughtless Charlie got his fist in?
How daddie Burke the plea was cooking,
If Warren Hastings' neck was itching;
If cesses dues, and fees were axed,
Or if bare bottoms yet were taxed:
The news of princes, dukes and earls,
Pimps and ponces, wayward girls.
If that daft fellow, Geordie Wales,     *Prince.*
Was chasing after hussies' tails,
Of if he's grown a little sober,

And not the perfect princely loafer.
All this and more I never heard of,
So gratefully back your news I send you,
And pray all good things may attend you.

Ellisland, Monday morning, 1790.

## THE GOLDEN LOCKS OF ANNA

Last night I sipped the sweetest wine,
Where none but we did wander;
Last night lay on this breast of mine
The golden locks of Anna.
The hungry Jew in wilderness
Rejoicing o'er his manna,
Was nothing to the honeyed bliss
Upon the lips of Anna.

You monarchs take the east and west,
From India to Savannah;
Give me within my straining grasp
The melting form of Anna.
There I'll despise imperial charms,
Of Empress or Sultana;
While dying raptures in her arms
I give and take with Anna.

Away, thou flaunting god of day;
Away, thou pale Diana;
And every star deflect thy ray
When I'm to meet my Anna.
Come, in thy raven plumage, night:
Sun, moon, and stars do not forgather,
And bring my lyric pen to write
My transports with my Anna.

This song was excluded from a contemporary publication,
in pique Burns added this postscript:-

The church and state may join and tell
Such things to do no longer:
The church and state may go to Hell,
And I'll go to my Anna.
She is the sunshine of my eye,
More fairer than Diana.
Had I on earth but wishes three,
The first would be with Anna.

## AFTON WATER

Flow gently, sweet Afton, among thy green braes,
Flow gently, I'll sing thee a song in thy praise.
My Mary's asleep by thy murmuring stream.
Flow gently, sweet Afton, disturb not her dream.

Thou stock-dove, whose echo resounds through the glen,
Ye wild whistling blackbirds in yon thorny den,
Thou green-crested lapwing thy screaming forbear,
I charge you disturb not my slumbering fair.

How lofty, sweet Afton, thy neighbouring hills,
Far marked with courses of clear winding rills.
There daily I wander as noon rises high,
My flocks and my Mary's sweet cot in my eye.

How pleasant thy banks and green valleys below,
Where wild in the woodland the primroses blow.
There oft as mild evening sweeps over the lea,
The sweet scented birches shade Mary and me.

Thy crystal stream Afton, how lovely it glides,
And winds by the cot where my Mary abides;
How wanton thy waters her snowy feet lave,      *Lap.*
As gathering sweet flowers she stems thy clear wave.

Thou stock-dove whose echo resounds through the glen,
You wild whistling blackbirds in yon thorny den,
Thou green-crested lapwing thy screaming forbear,
I charge you disturb not my slumbering fair.

## ADDRESS TO THE VERY GOOD

### Or the rigidly righteous

My son, these maxims make a rule,
And lump them all together;
The rigid righteous are but fools,
And rigid wise another:
The cleanest corn that e'er was born,
May have some bits of chaff in;
So ne'er a fellow mortal scorn,
For random fits of daffin.                    *Fun.*


Solomon. Eccles. vii. 16.


O you who are so good yoursel',
So pious and so holy,
You've nought to do but mark and tell
Your neighbours faults and folly.
Whose life is like a well-run mill,
Supplied with ample water,
The heapéd hoppers always full,
With never fear of falter.


Hear me, you venerable corps,
As counsel for poor mortals,
Who frequent pass wise wisdom's door,
For senseless folly's portals;
I, for their thoughtless, careless sakes
Would here propose defences,
Their trivial tricks, their black mistakes,
Their failings and mischances.


You see your state with theirs compared,
Exchange would make you shudder.
But cast a moment's fair regard
What makes the mighty differ?
Discount what scant occasion gave,
That purity you pride in
Is like all other mortals', save
You're better at its hiding.

Think, when your castigating pulse
Gives now and then a wallop,
What ragings must his veins convulse
That still eternal gallop.
With wind and tide fair in your tail,
Right on you scud your sea-way;
But in the teeth of both to sail,
You'll get the strongest lee-way.


See Social Life and Glee sit down,
All joyous and unthinking,
Till, quite transformed, and now they're grown
Debauchery and Drinking.
O, would they stay to calculate
The eternal consequences;
Or your more dreaded Hell to state,
Damnation of expenses.


You high, exalted, virtuous dames,
Tied up in godly laces,
Before you give poor Frailty names,
Suppose a change of cases;
A dear loved lad, convenience snug,
A treacherous inclination –
But, let me whisper in your lug,
Perhaps you're past temptation.


Then gently scan your fellow man.
Still gentler sister woman;
Although they know they're doing wrong,
To step aside is human:
One point must still be greatly dark,
The moving why they do it:
And just as lamely can you mark
How far perhaps they'll rue it.

Who made the heart, 'tis He alone
Decidedly can try us;
He knows each chord – its various tone,
Each spring – its various bias:
Then at the balance let's be mute,                    *Judgement Day.*
We never can adjust it;
What's done we partly may compute,
But know not what's resisted.

## TO DAUNTON ME

A maiden's reply to the overtures of an elderly suitor.

The blood-red rose at Yule may blow,
The summer lilies bloom in snow;
The frost may freeze the deepest sea,
But no old man will ensnare me.

> To ensnare me, and me so young,
> With his false heart and flattering tongue,
> That is the thing you ne'er shall see:
> For no old man will ensnare me.

For all his meal and all his malt,
For all his beef and all his salt,
For all his gold and white monéy:
Still no old man will ensnare me.

Money may buy him cows and sheep,
Money may buy him farms to keep;
But not for goods and not for fee
I'd let an old man ensnare me.

He limps along with feet of lead,
Has toothless gums, an old bald head,
The drops drip down from red-rimmed eyes:
He'll not have me for all his lies.

## THE OLD FARMER'S NEW YEAR MORNING
## SALUTATION TO HIS OLD MARE MAGGIE

A poem full of pathos and reminiscences of thirty years' companionship between a farmer and his horse.

A good New Year I wish you, Maggie,
And here's some corn to make you merry;
Though now your back is low and saggy,
    I've seen the day
When you could trounce and with no hurry
    Both roan and bay.

Though now you're old, stiff, and crazy,
And your old hide's as white's a daisy,
I've seen thee dappled, sleek, and glazie,
    A bonnie gray.
The arms were strong that used to rein thee,
    Once in a day.

You once were in the foremost rank,
A filly full of style and swank,
A head held high with shapely shank,
    Just take my word;
You could have flown o'er any bank,
    Like any bird.

It's now some nine and twenty year
Since you were born to father's mare,
Then marriage placed you in my care,
    With fifty pounds;
Though it was small, 'twas all his gear,
    And you were sound.

When first I went to woo my Jenny,
You then were trotting with your mammy;
Though you were tricky, sly, and funny,
    You were not flighty,
Nor docile, but well-bred and dandy,
    Bland and friendly.

That day you pranced with equine pride
When you brought home my bonnie bride,
And sweet and graceful she did ride
      With maiden air;
The countryside I boasted wide
      For such a pair.

Though now you can but limp and totter,
Like salmon boats in wintry weather,
That day your speed no horse could better;
      Clean heels you showed,
And ran them all into the gutter;
      Pegasus-like you rode.

When you and I were full of mettle,
For fairground feed you would not settle;
How you would prance and raise your hackle
      To take the road;
The towns-folk jumped when by you rattled,
      With ne'er a goad.

When you were fed and I was mellow,         *Tipsy.*
We took the road just like a swallow;
At races you had ne'er a fellow
      To match your speed,
And every time you beat them hollow,
      You worthy steed.

The swifter spurts of hunting aces,
Would sometimes win them shorter races,
But six Scotch miles soon slackens paces,
      And makes them snort,
No whip or spur to pass their Graces,
      And bring them nought.

You're a noble beast, I will allow;
Your strength soon showed when at the plough;
The farmers round, we showed them how
      In good March weather
To turn six roods, for that I'll vow,         *1½ acres.*
      For days together.

You never gave but of your best,
And what you did you did with zest,
And spread out wide your well-filled chest,
       With strength and brawn,
Till bump and hillock, ridge and crest,
       Were smooth as lawn.

When frost lay long and snow lay deep,
And cajoled labour back to sleep,
I gave you corn in such a heap
       To make you fitter;
I knew, my Maggie, I would reap
       Your toil in summer.

In cart or car you never rested,
The steepest hill you always bested:
Your strain was smooth, long hauls you faced it,
       Then stood to blow;
Each task you took you were well-tested,
       We all well know.

My ploughing team are now my bairns,
Four gallant brutes, short of brains;
Forbye six more I've sold for gains,
       You were their nurse.
Thirteen pounds for all my pains,
       What could be worse?

The weary work we two have wrought,
And with the weary world we fought,
And many an anxious day I thought
       We would be beat.
Yet here, to weary age we're brought,
       With something yet.

But think not, my old and trusty servant,
That now perhaps you're less deserving,
And your old days may end in starving;
       Before I go                                    *Die.*
I'll see you'll get your fairin                    *Rewards.*
       Laid by for you.

We've worn to weary years together;
We'll totter round with one another;
With tender care I'll fix your tether
    In grasses green
Where you can browse and stretch your leather††
    And reign a queen.

††Leather is horses' hide, therefore to stretch it means to eat to satiation.

This poem required 151 marginal words of explanation in Blackie's edition of 1887. This 'translation' has reduced them to 5 without, I trust, diverging from the original meaning.

## TO A PAINTER

This advice was given, gratis, to a friend whom Burns found painting a celestial scene.

Dear sir, I'll give you some advice,
You'll take it not uncivil,
You should not paint at angels,
But try and paint the Devil.
To paint an angel is tricky work,
With the Devil there's less danger;
You'll easily draw a well-known face,
But not so well a stranger.

## WHEN I THINK ON THE HAPPY DAYS

When I think on the happy days,
I spent with you my dearie,
And now what lands between us lie,
How can I be but eerie?

How slow you move, you heavy hours,
So slow, so slow, so weary;
It was not so you flitted by
When I was with my dearie.

## DEATH AND DOCTOR HORNBOOK

A true story.

John Wilson, Esq. of Tarbolton, combined the three voca-
tions of schoolmaster, grocer and quack doctor. His practising
of the latter often resulted in him complementing Death,
who took aversion to this rival.

The pseudonym was so obvious that Mr. Wilson was obliged
to quit the locality.


Some books are lies from end to end,
And some great lies were never penned.
Even ministers, they have been kenned,            *Known.*
  In holy rapture,
A rousing lie at times to vend,
  And blame the scripture.


But this that I am going to tell,
Which lately on a night befell,
Is just as true as the Devils in Hell
  Or Dublin city:            *A carving.*
That e'er he nearer comes oursel'.
  The more's the pity.


The village still had made me drowsy;
I was not drunk, but just had plenty;
I staggered, stumbled, but took care
  To clear the ditches,
And ascertained they weren't the lair
  Of howling ghosts and witches.


The rising moon began to glower
The distant Cumnock Hills o'er yonder:
To count her horns, with all my power
  I set mysel';
But whether it was three or four,
  I could not tell.

I was come round about the hill,
And toddling down on Willie's mill,
Setting my staff with all my skill,
  To keep me steady:
And leeward leaning 'gainst my will,
  Beheld a sight uncanny.

I there with Something did forgather,
That put me in a fearful dither;
An awful scythe across one shoulder,
  Clear dangling, hang;
A three-pronged spear across the other
  Lay large and lang.

Its stature seemed 'bout nine feet high,
A queerer shape I ne'er did spy,
With belly like a pregnant kye      *Cow.*
  And then its legs
Were thin and spindly (and set awry),
  Like wooden pegs.

'Good evening, sir,' quoth I, 'have you been mowing
When other folks are busy sowing?'
It seemed as It had nought to say,
  For speech was lack:
At length says I, 'Sir, whence your way
  Will you go back?'

It spoke right low, 'My name is Death
Be not afraid', Quoth I, 'Good faith,
Perhaps you've come to stop my breath
  And take my life;
I warn you well, do me no harm
  For I've a knife.'

'Good man,' quoth he, 'no need for knives,
I've no designs on human lives,
Nor have I any need for scythes
  For yet awhile;
So hold your hand till dawn arrives,
  And rest meanwhile.'

'Well, well,' says I, 'a bargain be it;
Shake my hand, and so we'll seal it;
Just take a seat and ease our load.
          Come now, what's the news?
This while you've been up many a road,
          At many a house.'

'It's true,' quoth he and shook his head,
'It's been a long, long time indeed
Since I began to cut the thread,
          And choke the breath:
Folk must do something for their bread,
          And mine is Death.'

'Six thousand years are nearly fled
Since I was to the slaughter bred,
And many a scheme in vain's been laid
          To stop or scare me;
Now Hornbook's taken up my trade,
          And faith he'll beat me.'

'You'll know Jock Hornbook in the village?
Before he's through I'll just be silage.
He reads mysterious doctors books;
          Such cures he does attempt,
The children leer with laughing looks,
          Their fingers show contempt.'

'See, here's a scythe, and there's a dart
That's pierced so many a gallant heart;
But Doctor Hornbrook, with his skill
          And curséd art,
Has made them both unfit to kill,
          Blast be his part.'

'Twas just last night, just at sundown,
I threw a thrustful throw at one;
With lesser care I've hundreds slain;
          But, woe's my lot;
I'm proved a lesser man than Cain.
          I missed my shot.'

'Hornbrook was near, with ready art,
And had so fortified the part
That when I lookéd to my dart
        It was so blunt
It would never have pierced the heart
        Of a rotten cabbage stump.'

'I drew my scythe in such a fury
I nearly tumbled in my hurry,
But yet the bold apothecary
        Withstood the shock;
I might as well have tried to quarry
        Granite rock.'

'Even those folks he can't attend,
And those whose face he never kenned,                    *Knew.*
Their symptoms in a letter send
        And by return
Are sent the cure their ills to mend;
        Too late they learn.'

'And then all doctors' saws and whittles,                *Knives.*
Of all dimensions, shapes, and mettles,
All kinds of boxes, mugs and bottles,
        He has for ye,
Their Latin names he reels and rattles
        As A B C.'

'Calces of fossils, earths and trees;
True *sal-marinum* of the seas;
The farina of beans and peas,
        He has in plenty;
*Aqua-fortis*, what you please,
        He can content ye.'

'Forbye some new, uncommon weapons,
*Urinus spiritus* of capons;
Or mite horn shavings, fillings, scrapings,
        Distilled *per se;*
*Sal-alkali* of midge-tail clippings,
        All these has he.'

'Woe is me I'm for my grave,'
Quoth I, 'if that sad news be true.'
This neat graveyard where daisies grew,
    So white and bonnie,
No doubt they'll tear it with the plough
    And ruin Johnnie.'          *Gravedigger.*

The creature gave a screaming laugh,
And says, 'You need not yoke the plough,
Graveyards will soon be tilled somehow,
    Take you no fear:
They'll all be trenched, and if not now,
    In two three year.'

'Where I killed one in lawful death,
By loss of blood or want of breath,
I'll take my oath and shout aloud,
    That Hornbook's skill
Has placed a score within their shroud,
    By dose and pill.'

'An honest weaver to his trade,
Whose wife was once a gentle maid,
Got two-pence worth to mend her head,
    When it was sore;
The wife slid gently down the bed,
    But spoke no more.'

'A country laird was down with bots,          *Botulism.*
With awful pain within his guts,
His only son for Hornbook sallies forth,
    And pays him well.
The lad, for two good guineas worth,
    Was laird himsel'.'

'A bonnie lass, you know her name;
(Some ill-bred youth should take the blame),
She trusts herself, to hide her shame,
    In Hornbook's care,
Horn sent her to her heavenly hame,
    To hide it there.'

'That's just a batch of Hornbook's way,
Thus goes he on from day to day
Thus does he poison, kill, and slay,
        For he's a quack,
Yet stops me of my lawful prey,
        With his damned muck.'

'But hark, I'll tell you of a plot,
Now don't you go and spoil the lot,
I'll nail that self-conceited sot
        As dead as meat:
He'll get his dues, I'll bet a groat,
        Next time we meet.'

But just as he began to tell,
The old church-hammer struck the bell
Some small short hour past the twelve,
        Which raised us both:
I took the way that pleased mysel',
        And so did Death.

## VERSES TO A LANDLADY

My blessings on you, my good wife,
I ne'er was here before,
You've given us much for fork and knife,
None could wish for more.
Heaven keep you from care and strife,
Till far beyond fourscore,
And, while I toddle on through life,
I'll ne'er go past your door.

# ADDRESS TO THE TOOTHACHE

My curse upon your venomed sting,
That makes my tortured gums to sing
With melodies from out of hell,
    With gnawing vengeance;
Tearing my nerves both taught and fell,
    Like racking engines.


When fevers burn, or ague freezes,
Rheumatics gnaw, or cholic squeezes,
Our neighbours' sympathy may ease us,
    With pitying moan;
But thou – thou Hell of all diseases –
    Just mocks our groan.


All down my beard saliva flows,
I kick at doors to stem my woes,
As giggling girls no pity shows;
    To see me leap,
While raving mad, I wish a barb
    Was in their seat.


Of all the numerous human ills,
Ill-fortune, daft bargains, bankrupt mills,
Or worthy friends too soon departed
    No more to rise,
The tricks of knaves, slandering quills,
    You'll get the prize.


Where'er the place the priests call Hell,
Whence all the tones of misery yell,
And rankéd plaques their numbers tell,
    In dreadfull pall,
Thou, toothache, will always dwell,
    Above them all.

O thou grim, mischief-making pain
That drives a man almost insane,
'Gainst cures that all have been in vain,
    For misery's sake
Give all those seeking Scotland's wane,
    A year's toothache.

## THE RUINED MAID'S LAMENT

Oh, sadly do I rue false love,
Oh, sadly do I rue,
That e'er I heard your flattering tongue,
That e'er your face I knew.

Oh, I have lost my rosy cheeks,
Likewise my waist so small;
And I have lost my lightsome heart,
That cannot bear the gall.

Now I must bear the scornful sneer
Of many a saucy quean,
When if the truth were only known,
Her life's been worse than mine.

Whene'er my father thinks on me,
He stares into the wall;
My mother's taken to her bed,
Through thinking of my fall.

Whene'er I hear my father's foot,
My heart would burst with pain;
Whene'er I meet my mother's eyes,
My tears come down like rain.

Alas, so sweet a tree as love
Such bitter fruit should bear;
Alas, that e'er a pretty face
Should show a salty tear.

But Heaven's curse will blast the man
Who denies the child he got,
Or leaves the ruined lass he loved
To her sad and shameful lot.

## AE FOND KISS

This song is deemed to be the essence of the poet's romantic sensibilities, knowing he could never attain their fulfilment.

One fond kiss, and then we sever;
One farewell, and then for ever.
Deep in heart-rung tears I'll pledge thee,
Warring sighs and groans I'll wage thee.
Who shall say that Fortune grieves him
While the star of hope she leaves him?
Me, no cheerful twinkle lights me;
Dark despair around benights me.

I'll never blame my partial fancy,
Nothing could resist my Nancy;
But to see her was to love her;
Love but her, and love for ever.
Had we never loved so kindly,
Had we never loved so blindly,
Never met, and never parted,
We had ne'er been broken-hearted.

Fare thee well, my first and fairest,
Fare thee well, thou blest and dearest.
Thine be every joy and treasure,
Peace, enjoyment, love and pleasure.
One fond kiss and then we sever;
One farewell, alas, for ever;
Deep in heart-rung tears I'll pledge thee,
Warring sighs and groans I'll wage thee.

## A WINTER NIGHT

The poet, while snug and warm indoors on a bitter winter night, has thoughts on the creatures exposed to the storm without, and finds himself in tune with Shakespeare.

> Poor naked wretches, whereso'er you are,
> That bide the pelting of this pitiless storm,
> How shall your houseless heads and unfed sides,
> Your loop'd and windowed raggedness, defend you
> From seasons such as these?
>                 King Lear III iv 28

The bitter North, cold and dour,
Sends shivers through the leafless bower;
The sun sends forth a short-lived glower,
        Far south its lift,
Dim-glinting through the flaky shower,
        Or whirling drift.

One night the storm the steeples rocked;
Poor Labour sweet in sleep was locked,
While streams their seaward runs were blocked
        With eddying swirl,
Or through the mining outlet bocked,          *Gushed.*
        Down headlong hurl . . .

I heard the doors and windows rattle,
And I thought on the shivering cattle,
Or silly sheep that bear the battle
        Of winter war,
Or in a snowdrift settle,
        Beneath a scaur.                       *Cliff.*

Each hopping bird, wee helpless thing,
That in the merry months of spring,
Delighted me to hear you sing,
        What comes of thee?
Where will you cower your shivering wing
        And close your e'e?

Even you on murdering errands toiled,                    *Fox.*
Lone from the savage home exiled,
The blood-stained roost, the sheep-pen spoiled
  My heart forgets,
While pitiless the tempest wild
  Sore on you beats.


The silent moon in midnight reign
Dark muffled, viewed the dreary plain;
My crowding thoughts, a pensive train,
  Rose in my soul,
When on my ear the plaintive strain,
  Slow, solemn, stole:–


'Blow, blow, ye winds with heavier gust;
And freeze, thou bitter-biting frost;
Descend, ye chilly, smothering snows;
Not all your rage, as now united, shows
More hard unkindness, unrelenting,
Vengeful malice, unrepenting,
Than heaven-illumin'd man on brother man bestows.


See stern Oppression's iron grip,
Or mad Ambition's gory hand,
Sending, like blood-hounds from the slip,
Woe, want and murder o'er a land.
Even in the peaceful rural vale,
Truth, weeping, tells the mournful tale,
How pampered Luxury, Flattery by her side,
The parasite empoisoning her ear,
With all the servile wretches in the rear,
Looks o'er proud property, extended wide;
And eyes the simple rustic hind,                    *Farm worker.*
Whose toil upholds the glittering show,
A creature of another kind,
Some coarser substance unrefined,
Placed for her lordly use thus far, thus vile below.


Where, where, is love's fond, tender throe,
With lordly Honour's lofty brow,
The powers you proudly own?

Is there, beneath Love's noble name,
Can harbour, dark, the selfish aim,
To bless himself alone?
Mark maiden-innocence a prey
To love-pretending snares,
This boasted Honour turns away,
Shunning soft Pity's rising sway,
Regardless of the tears, the unavailing prayers;
Perhaps, this hour, in misery's squalid nest
She strains your infant to her joyless breast,
And with a mother's fears shrinks at the rocking blast.

'Oh ye, who sunk in beds of down,
Feel not a want but what yourselves create,
Think, for a moment, on his wretched fate,
Whom friends and fortune quite disown,
Ill-satisfied keen nature's clamorous call;
Stretched on his bed of straw he lays himself to sleep,
While through the ragged roof, and chinky wall,
Chill o'er his slumbers piles the drifty heap;
Think on the dungeon's grim confine,
Where guilt and poor misfortune pine;
Guilt, erring man, relenting view,
But shall the legal rage pursue
The wretch, already crushéd low
By cruel fortune's undeservéd blow?
Affliction's sons are brothers in distress,
A brother to relieve, how exquisite the bliss!'

I heard no more, for Chanticleer,              *Rooster, Cock.*
Shook off the powdery snow,
And hailed the morning with a cheer,
A cottage-rousing crow.

But deep this truth impressed my mind,
Through all His works abroad,
The heart, benevolent and kind,
The most resembles God.

## OH, AYE, MY WIFE SHE DANG ME       *Beat*

Oh, aye my wife o'ercame me,
And now she often crowns me,
Just let a woman have her will,
Good faith, she'll soon overcome you.
On peace and rest my mind was bent,
And fool I was I married;
But ne'er was honest man's intent
As cursedly miscarried.
I draw some comfort still at last,
When all my days are ended,
My pains of Hell on earth are passed,
Above they'll all be mended.

## THE TARBOLTON LASSES

This, and the next poem, 'The Ronalds': extols the virtues and graces of the eligible young ladies of the Parish. Sheer penury forbids our poet to risk any amorous advances.

If you go up to yon hill-top,
You'll see there bonnie Peggy;
She knows her father is a laird,                    *Land-owner.*
And she's forsooth a lady.

There's Sophy tight, a lassie bright,
Besides a handsome fortune;
Who cannot win her in a night
Has little art in courting.

Go down by Faile and taste the ale,
And take a look at Maisy;
She's dour and dim, a devil within,
Perhaps she'll aim to please ye.

If she be shy her sister try,
You'll maybe fancy Jenny;
If you'll dispense with want of sense,
She knows herself she's bonnie.

As you go up by yon hillside,
Look out for bonnie Bessie,
With curtesy low, she'll make a show,
And handsomely address ye.

There's few so bonnie, none so good,
In all King George's Kingdom;
If you should doubt the truth of this,
It's Bessie's own opinion.

## THE RONALDS

In Tarbolton, ye ken, there are proper young men,
And proper young lasses and all, man;
But know ye the Ronalds that live in the Bennels;
They're the pick of the bunch of them all, man.

Their father's a laird, and well he can spare it,
Good money to marry them all, man;
To proper young men he'll clink in his hand,
Gold guineas a hundred or two, man.

There's one they call Jean, I'll warrant you've seen
No bonnier a lass or as sweet, man,
For sense and good taste, she'll vie with the best,
And a conduct that beautifies all, man.

The charms of their minds, a lad always finds,
A permanent admiration;
While peaches and cherries, and roses and lilies,
They fade and they wither away, man.

If you're for Miss Jean, take this from a friend,
You've a rival or two for the prize, man.
The laird of Blackbyre would go through the fire,
If that would entice her away, man.

The laird of Braehead would stand on his head
For more than a twelvemonth or two, man;
The laird of the Ford will die by his sword,
If he cannot get her at all, man.

Then Anna comes in, the pride of her kin,
The boast of our bachelors all, man;
So saucy but sweet, so fully complete,
She steals our affections away, man.

I love her myself, but dare not explain;
My poverty keeps me in awe, man.
For making of rhymes, and working at times,
Earns little or nothing at all, man.

Yet I wouldn't choose to let her refuse
To give her the power to say no, man.
For though I be poor, unnoticed, obscure,
My stomach's as proud as them all, man.

Though I cannot ride in well-booted pride,
And fly o'er the hills like a crow, man,
I can hold up my head, so let it be said;
I can dress like a lord when I try, man.

My coat and my vest, they are Scotch of the best,
Of pairs of good pants I have two, man;
And stockings and pumps to put on my stumps,
And ne'er a wrong stitch in them all, man.

My shirts they are few, but five of them new,
As fine and as white as the snowman;
A ten-shilling hat, a Holland cravat,
My finery leaves them in awe, man.

I never had friends with overstocked means
To leave me a hundred or two, man;
No wealthy old aunts, to tend on their wants,
And wish them in Hell for it all, man.

I never was careful for hoarding of money,
Or of gathering of filthy lucre;
I've little to spend, and nothing to lend,
But never a shilling I owe, man.

## BEWARE O' BONNIE ANN

You gallants bright, I warn you right,
Beware of bonnie Ann;
Her comely face, so full of grace,
Your heart she will trepan.
Her eyes so bright, like stars at night;
Her skin is like the swan;
So tightly laced, her waspish waist,
That sweetly you might span.

Youth, grace, and love attendant move,
And pleasure leads the van,
In all their charms and conquering arms,
They wait on bonnie Ann.
The captive bands may chain the hands,
But love enslaves the man;
You gallants bright, I warn you right,
Beware of bonnie Ann.

# THE AUTHOR'S EARNEST CRY AND PRAYER,
## TO THE SCOTCH REPRESENTATIVES
## IN THE HOUSE OF COMMONS

The theme of this poem touches on a raw nerve of all
Scotsmen – the price of whisky.

You Irish lords, you knights and squires,
Who represent our towns and shires,
And wisely manage our affairs
    In parliament,
To you a simple poet's prayers
    Are humbly sent.

Alas, my muted muse is hoarse,
Your honours' hearts with grief would pierce,
To hear her spouting out her curse,
    Low in the dust,
And screeching out prosaic verse,
    As if to burst.

Tell them who have the chief direction,
Scotland and me's in great affliction,
Ever since they laid that cursed restriction
    On Scottish whisky;
And rouse them up to strong conviction,
    And move their pity.

Stand forth, and tell yon Premier Youth,        *Mr. Pitt.*
The honest, open, naked truth;
Tell him of mine and Scotland's drought,
    His servants humble:
The vengeful Devil blow you south,        *To England.*
    If you dissemble.

Does any great man fudge and frown,
To speak out loud and bang his drum?
Let posts and pensions sink or boom
    With them that grant them,
If honestly they cannot come,
    Far better want them.

In gathering votes you were not slack.
Now stand up straight, keep to your tack;
Don't scratch your ear or shrug your back,
     And hum and haw;
But raise your arm, no courage lack
     Before them a'.

Paint Scotland crying o'er her thistle,
Her pint-pot emptied without a tussle,
And damned Excise men in a bustle
     Seizing a still,
Triumphant crushing it like a mussel
     Or limpet shell.

Then on the other hand present her
A blackguard smuggler right behind her,
And cheek by jowl, a fat-faced vintner
     Conspiring join,
Picking her purse as bare as winter
     Of all her coin.

Is there, that bears the name of Scot,
But feels his heart's blood rising hot,
To see his poor old mother's pot
     With broken staves,
And plundered of her hindmost groat
     By gallows knaves?

Alas, I'm but a nameless wight,
Trod in the mire out of sight,
But could I like a soldier fight,
     And talk and tell,
There's some neckties I would draw tight,
     And tie the knot as well.

God bless your honours, but hear the bleat
Of kind old housewives as they greet;          *Cry.*
So get up warmly on your feet,
     And make them hear it,
And tell them, with patriotic heat,
     You will not stand it.

Some of you know full well the laws,
To round the period and the pause,
And with rhetoric clause on clause
    To make harangues;
Then echo through St. Stephen's walls     *Parliament.*
    Old Scotland's wrongs.

Dempster, a true blue Scot of learning,
Thee, oath-detesting, chaste Kilkerran;
And that smooth tongued Highland baron,
    The lord of Graham,
And one, a chap that's damned o'erbearing,
    Dundas his name.

Erskine, a lively Northland fellow;
True Campbells, Frederick and Ilay;
And Livingstone, the bold Sir Willie;
    And many others,
Whom old Demosthenes or Tully
    Might own for brothers.

Thee, soldier Hugh, I've oftimes hinted,
If poets are ever represented,
I know that if your sword was wanted
    You'd lend a hand;
But when there's ought to say about it,
    You're at a stand.     *Tongue-tied.*

Arouse, my boys, exert your mettle,
And put old Scotland back in fettle,
Or faith, I'll pawn my new plough-pettle,
    You'll see it ere long.
She'll teach thee like a scalding kettle,
    Another song.

This while she's been in fractious mood,
Proposed conscription fired her blood,
The Devil himself could do more good
    With plans so risky,
And now your tricks come in a flood,
    About her whisky.

If you accuse her once of guilt,
Her tartan petticoat she'll kilt,
With dirk and pistol at her belt
        She'll take the streets,
And run her dirk up to the hilt,
        The first she meets.

For God's sake, sirs, then speak her fair,
And gently stroke her silken hair,
Thence to Parliament repair
        With instant speed,
And strive, without ne'er a thought of fear,
        To get remead.

That ill-tongued tinker, Charlie Fox,        *English Statesman.*
May taunt you with his jeers and mocks,
But give him Hell, my hearty cocks
        With ought that's handy,
And send him to his dicing box
        And sporting lady.

Tell yon good blood of old Boconnóck's        *Premier Wm. Pitt.*
I'll owe him two good Scottish bannocks,
And drink his health in Nancy Tinnock's        *Tavern.*
        Nine times a week,
If he some scheme, like tea and winnocks,        *Windows.*
        Would kindly seek.

Could he some commutation broach,
I'll pledge my oath in good broad Scotch;
He need not fear their foul reproach
        Nor erudition;
Eschew that nasty queer hotch-potch,
        The coalition.

Old Scotland had a fearless tongue,
Sometimes a devil with a prong,
And if she promise old or young
        To take their part,
Though by the neck she should be strung,
        She'll not desert.

And now you chosen five and forty,                    *M.P's.*
May still your mother's heart support ye,
And though a Minister may hurt ye
          And insult your Race,
You'll snap your fingers hard and hearty,
          Before his face.

God bless your honours all your days,
With lots of broth and plenty clothes,
In spite of all their knavish ways
          That haunt St. James,                    *British Court.*
Your humble poet sings and prays
          While Rab his name is.

## POSTSCRIPT

Let half-starved slaves in warmer skies
See future wines, rich clust'ring, rise.
Their lot old Scotland ne'er envies,
        But, blythe and frisky,
She sees her freeborn, martial boys
        Take oft their whisky.


What though their sunshine kinder warms,
While fragrance blooms and beauty charms,
When wretches range, in famished swarms
        The scented groves,
Or hounded forth, dishonour arms
        In hungry droves.


Their gun's a burden on their shoulder,
They cannot stand the smell of powder.
The boldest thoughts a doubting dither
        To stand or run,
The opening shot will send them thither
        To save their skin.


But, bring a Scotsman from his hill,
Put in his hand a Highland gill,
Say, such is royal George's will,
        And there's the foe,
He has no thought but how to kill,
        Two at a blow.


No cold, faint-hearted doubtings tease him,
Death comes, with fearless eyes he sees him;
With bloody hand a welcome gives him:
        And when he falls,
His latest draught of breathing leaves him,
        In faint hurrahs.

Sages with solemn eyes will seek,
To raise a philosophic reason weak,
Search for causes that are bleak,
  In clime and season;
But tell me whisky's name in Greek,
  I'll tell the reason.

Scotland, my old respected mother,
It's no use sitting about on heather,
You'll only wet your clothes and shiver,
  And lose respect,
Freedom and whisky go together;
  On that reflect.         +

 + The authority for the 'translation' of the last verse is to
be found in Brewer's Dictionary of Phrase and Fable.

## MY OWN KIND DEARIE

When o'er the hill the eastern star,
Brings maids unto their dairy,
The cattle from the fields afar,
Return so full and weary;
Down by the stream where scented birch
With dew are hanging clearly,
I'll meet thee by the trysting tree,
My own kind dearie.

In darkest glen, at midnight hour,
I'd rove and ne'er be eerie,
If through the glen I came to thee,
My own kind dearie.
Although the night were e'er so wild,
And I were ne'er so weary,
I'd meet thee by the trysting tree,
My own kind dearie.

The hunter loves the morning sun,
To rouse the mountain deer;
At noon the fisher seeks the stream,
Along its course to steer.
Give me the hour of gloaming time;
It makes my heart so cheery
To meet thee by the trysting tree,
My own kind dearie.

# HAD I THE WYTE

## (Was I to blame?)

Was I to blame? was I to blame?
Was I to blame she lured me?
She waited on the main highway,
Then up the lane she led me;
And when I wouldn't venture in,
A coward fool she called me:
Had Church and State been at that gate,
They neither could have stopped me.

So craftily she led me in,
And bade me make no clatter,
For her brutal bawdy sailor man,
Was away upon the water.
Whoe'er shall say I wanted grace,
When I did kiss and hold her,
Let him be planted in my place,
And see if he would falter.

Could I for shame, could I for shame,
Could I for shame refuse her?
My manhood would have been to blame,
Had I not amused her.
When such a husband is from home,
What wife but would excuse her?
He's clawed her almost to the bone,
And black and blue he's bruised her.

I wiped her eyes of bonny blue,
(She blamed her man so randy)
And when I met her willing lips,
'Twas like a sugar candy.
'Twas gloaming time as I recall,
It was upon a Monday,
And I walked through the Tuesday's dew,
With that brutal sailor's brandy.

## MY LADY'S GOWN

My lady's gown, there's frills upon it,
And golden flowers so rare upon it,
But Jenny's dress of homespun cloth,
My lord he thinks the more upon it.

My lord a-hunting he has gone,
But hounds and hawks he has not one.
In Collin's cottage lies his game,
If Collin's Jenny be at hame.

My lady's white, my lady's red,
And kith and kin with all the lairds.
Her dowry gold made them well paired,
And that was all his lairdship cared.

Out o'er the moor, out o'er the moss,
Where game-birds through the heather pass,
There dwells old Collin's bonny lass,
A lily in the wilderness.

So sweetly move her gentle limbs,
Like music notes of lover's hymns,
The diamond dew in eyes so blue,
Where laughing love so wanton swims.

My lady's neat, my lady's dressed,
The flower and fancy of the west;
But the lassie that a man loves best,
Oh, that's the lass to make him blest.

## HOLY WILLIE'S PRAYER

Bachelor William Fisher, alias Holy Willie, was instrumental in arraigning Burns' friend Gavin Hamilton before the Church Session on allegations proved groundless by his advocate Robert Aiken. Holy Willie was himself hypocrytical in his religious beliefs. Burns directed this satire against him.

O Thou who in the heaven does dwell,
Who, as it pleases best thysel',
Sends one to Heaven and ten to Hell,
    All for thy glory,
And not for any good or ill,
    They've done afore thee.

I bless and praise Thy matchless might,
When thousands you have left in night,
That I am here, before Thy sight,
    For gifts of grace,
A burning and a shining light,
    To all this place.

What was I, or my generation,
That I should get such exaltation;
I, who deserve Thy just damnation,
    For broken laws,
Five thousand years 'fore my creation,
    Through Adam's cause.

When from my mothers womb I fell,
Thou might have plunged me into Hell,
To gnash my bones, to weep and wail,
    In burning lakes,
Where all damned devils roar and yell,
    Chained to their stakes.

Yet I am here, a chosen sample,
To show Thy grace is great and ample;
I'm here a pillar of Thy temple,
    Strong as a rock,
A guide, a buckler, an example
    To all Thy flock.

O Lord, thou knows what zeal I bear
When drinkers drink, and swearers swear,
And dancing here, and singing there,
  With great and small;
From these I'm kept by mortal fear,
  Free from them all.

But yet, O Lord, confess I must,
At times I think of fleshly lust,
And sometimes, too, with worldly trust,
  Vile self gets in;
But thou remembers we are dust,
  Defiled in sin.

O Lord, last night, you know, with Meg,
Thy pardon I sincerely beg,
Oh, may it ne'er be a living plague,
  To my dishonour,
I'll never lift a lawless leg,
  Again upon her.

Besides, I further must allow,
With Lizzie's lass, three times I vow –
But Lord, last Friday I was fou'.       *Drunk.*
  Of this I tell you now,
Or else, you know, thy servant true,
  Would ne'er molest her.

Maybe Thou lets this fleshly thorn
Beset Thy servant e'en and morn,
Lest he o'er high and proud should turn,
  Because he is so gifted.
If so, Thy hand must e'er be borne,
  Until Thou lift it.

Lord, bless Thy chosen in this place,
For here Thou has a chosen race;
But God confound their stubborn face,
  And blast their name,
Who bring their elders to disgrace,
  And public shame.

Lord, give Hamilton his just deserts;
He drinks, and swears, and plays at cards,
Yet has so many taking arts,
  Both great and small,
From God's own priests and people's hearts,
  He steals them all.

And when we chastened him therefore,
Thou knows he made a great furore,
And sent the whole world in a roar
  Of laughing at us,
Curse Thou his victuals and his store
  Of cabbage and potatoes.

Lord, hear my earnest cry and prayer,.
Against the Presbyt'ry of Ayr;
Thy strong right hand, make it bear,
  Upon their heads.
Lord, weigh it down, and do not spare,
  For their misdeeds.

O Lord my God, that glib tongued Aiken,
My very heart and soul were shaking,
To think how we stood groaning, shaking,
  And sweat with dread,
While Auld with hanging lip and faces making,   *The Rev.*
  He hung his head.

Lord, in the day of vengeance try him;
Lord, visit them that did employ him,
And pass not in Thy mercy by them,
  Nor hear their prayer;
But for thy people's sake destroy them,
  And do not spare.

But, Lord, remember me and mine,
With mercies temporal and divine,
That I for wealth and grace may shine,
  Excelled by none,
And all the glory shall be Thine,
  Amen, amen.

## EPITAPH ON HOLY WILLIE

Here Holy Willie's sore worn clay,
Takes up its last abode,
His soul has taken some other way,
I fear the left hand road.

Stop: there he is, as sure's a gun;
Poor silly body, see him.
No wonder he's as black as they come,
Observe who's standing with him.

Your brimstone Devilship I see,
You've got him there before you;
But hold your nine-tailed cat a wee,
Till once you've heard my story.

Your pity I will not implore,
For pity you have none.
Justice, alas, has given him o'er,
And mercy's day is gone.

But hear me, Devil as you are,
Look something to your credit;
A fool like him would stain your name,
If it were known you did it.

## FOR ALL THAT AND ALL THAT

This poem/song expresses, perhaps above all others, Burns'
view of contemporary life, with his idealistic hope for the
future.

Is there for honest Poverty,
That hangs his head and all that?
The coward slave, we pass him by,
We dare be poor for all that.
For all that, and all that,
Our toil's obscure, and all that,
The rank is but the guinea's stamp,
The man's the gold for all that.

What though on homely fare we dine,
Wear homespun clothes and all that?
Give fools their silks, and knaves their wine,
A man's a man for all that.
For all that and all that,
Their tinsel show and all that,
The honest man, though e'er so poor,
Is king of men for all that.

You see yon fledgling called a lord,
Who struts, and stares, and all that?
Though hundreds worship at his word,
He's but a fool for all that.
For all that, and all that,
His ribbon, star, and all that.
The man of independent mind,
He looks and laughs at all that.

A king can make a belted knight,
A marquis, duke, and all that,
But an honest man, he knows what's right;
Good faith, he'll rise above that.
For all that and all that,
Their dignities, and all that,
The pride of sense, the pride of worth,
Are higher ranks than all that.

Then let us pray that come it may –
As come it will for all that,
That sense and worth o'er all the earth,
Will always be the hall-mark.
For all that, and all that,
It's coming yet for all that,
That man to man, the world o'er,
Shall brothers be for all that.

## SCOTCH DRINK

Give him Scotch drink, until he wink,
    That's sinking in despair,
And liquor good to fire his blood,
    That's pressed with grief and care;
There let him booze, and deep carouse,
    With glasses flowing o'er,
Till he forgets his loves and debts,
    And minds his griefs no more.

Solomon's Proverbs, xxxi 6, 7.

Let other poets raise a fracas,
'Bout vines and wines, and drunken Bacchus,
With poems and stories that torment us,
        And grate our ear.
I praise the juice Scotch barley gives us,
        That lifts our fear.

O thou, my muse, good old Scotch drink,          *Whisky.*
Squeezed through retorts of many a link,
Or, richly brown, ream o'er the brink,           *Beer.*
        In glorious foam,
Inspire me, till I lisp and wink,
        To sing thy name.

Let husky wheat the fields adorn,
And oats to ripen in the sun,
And peas and beans, at e'en and morn,
        Perfume the plain;
Commend to me John Barleycorn,
        Thou king of grain.

On thee oft Scotland chews the cud,
On supple scones, the choicest food,
Or tumbling in the boiling flood,                *Broth.*
        With kale and beef:
But when thou pours thy strong heart's blood,
        There thou shines chief.

Food fills us full, and keeps us living,
Though life's a gift not worth receiving
When overcome with pain and grieving;
    But, oiled by thee,
The wheels of life go downhill gliding,
    With merry glee.

Thou clears the head of doubting Fear,
Thou clears the head of drooping Care,
Thou soothes the nerves of Labour sair            *Sore.*
    Who weary toil;
Thou even brightens dark Despair,
    With gloomy smile.

You're often served in silver cup,
To gentry show thy foaming head,
Yet humble folk they also sup,
    The poor man's wine,
And in his porridge, or on his bread,
    Thou savours fine.

Thou art the life of public haunts,
Without thee what are fairs and rants,
Even godly meetings of the saints,
    By thee inspired,
When gaping they besiege the tents,        *See 'The Holy Fair'.*
    Are doubly fired.

That merry night we get the corn in,
The world seems sweeter to be born in,
Or reeking on a New-year morning,
    In glass or beaker,
With whisky mixed to get us reeling,
    And tasty sugar.

When Vulcan gives his bellows breath,
And ploughmen gather with their graith,      *Implements.*
O rare, to see thee fizz and froth,
    In amber glow;
The blacksmith shows his fiery wrath,
    In every blow.

No mercy, then, for iron or steel,
The brawny blacksmith shows his weal,
Brings hard o'er hip, with sturdy wheel,
  The strong sledge-hammer,
Till block and anvil ring and reel,
  With dinsome clamour.

When crying babies see the light,
Thou makes the gossips chatter bright,
The fickle females men-folk slight,
  'They're all the same.'
No midwife gets a social night,
  Or fee from them.

When neighbours quarrel for all to see,
Are just as mad as mad can be,
The barley-brew for referee
  Cements the quarrel.
It's cheaper than a lawyer's fee,
  To broach a barrel.

Alas, that e'er my muse has reason
To blame her country men of treason,
With foreign liquors have a craze on,
  And friends entice,
And hardly, in a winter's season,
  Enquire the price.

What worth is brandy, burning trash,
Fell source of choleras that harass,
Bereaving stupid men so brash,
  Of half their days,
And sends, besides, good Scottish cash,
  To her worst foes.

You Scots, who wish old Scotland well,
You chief, to you my tale I'll tell.
Poor penniless devils like mysel'
  It sets you ill,
With bitter pricey wines to deal,
  Or foreign gill.

May gravels round his bladder wrench,
And gout torment him inch by inch,
And twists his face with many a pinch
      Of sour disdain,
Despising a glass of whisky punch
      With honest men.

O whisky, soul of plays and pranks,
Accept a poet's grateful thanks,
When wanting thee, what tuneless cranks
      Are my poor verses.
Thou comes – there's joy within the ranks
      And no more curses.

Thee, Ferintosh; O sadly lost,
Scotland, lament from coast to coast,
Colics and coughing surely must
      Soon kill us all;
For royal Forbes' chartered boast,               ++
      Has come to fall.

The cursed horse-leeches of the Excise,
Who make the whisky stills their prize,
Hold up thy hand, Devil, once, twice, thrice.
      There, seize the blinkers,
And bake them up in brimstone pies,
      For poor damned drinkers.

Fortune; if you will give me still,
Good pants, a scone, a whisky gill,
And reams of rhymes to rave at will,
      Take all the rest,
And dole them out as thy blind skill
      Directs the best.

++Forbes of Ferintosh, distiller of whisky, was deprived of
his freedom from Excise Duty.

## TIBBIE I HAE SEEN THE DAY

Burns composed this song at the age of 17.

Oh, Tibbie, I have seen the day
You wouldn't have been so shy.
For lack of gold you slighted me,
But do I care? not I.

Today I met you on the moor,
You did not speak but passed like stoure. *Dust.*
You glared at me because I'm poor,
But not a hair care I.

When coming home on Sunday last
Upon the road as I came past,
You sniffed and gave your head a cast.
But, truth, I do not care.

I doubt not lass, but you may think
Because you make the sovereigns clink,
That you can please me with a wink,
When e'er you like to try.

But sorrow take him that's so mean,
Although his purse of coin is clean.
Who follows any saucy quean,
That looks so proud and high?

Although a lad was over smart,
And hankered for your golden dirt,
You'll turn your head and treat him curt,
And leave him high and dry.

But if he has both gold and gear,
You'll fasten to him like a brier,
Even though he's somewhat queer.
Tell me this, just why?

But, Tibbie lass, take my advice:
Your father's gold makes you so nice,
But not a one would ask your price,
Were you as poor as I.

There lives a lass I've lately found
I would not change, to her I'm bound,
For thee with all thy thousand pound,
So do not look so high.

## ADDRESS TO THE DEVIL

O Prince, O Chief of many throned powers,
That led th' embattled seraphim to war.
      Milton.


O Thou, whatever title suit thee,
Old Hornie, Satan, Nick or Clootie,
Who in your cavern grim and sootie,
      Closed under hatches,
Flinging your brimstone so unholy,
      To scald poor wretches.

Hear me, old Devil, forego that smile,
And let damned bodies rest awhile.
I'm sure small pleasure it affords,
      Even to a devil,
To scar and score with searing sword,
      The sons of evil.

Great is thy power, and great thy fame,
Far known and noted is thy name,
And though a burning pit's thy hame,
      Thou travels far,
And faith, thou's neither slow nor lame;
      The sea's no bar.

Whiles ranging like a roaring lion,
For prey at holes and corners lying,
Whiles on a strong-winged tempest flying,
      Unroofing churches,
Whiles in the human bosom prying,
      Unseen thou lurches.

I've heard my reverend grannie say
In lonely glens you like to stray,
Or where old ruined castles gray
      Nod to the moon.
You scare the wanderer's lonely way,
      With hideous croon.

When twilight did my grannie summon
To say her prayers, sweet sober woman,
Beyond the wall she's heard you humming,
        With eerie drone,
Or, rustling through the bushes coming
        With heavy groan.

One dreary, windy, winter night
The stars shot down with glancing light,
With you, myself, I got a fright.
        Down by the lake
You, like the rushes, stood in sight.
        You made me quake.

The cudgel in thy fist did shake,
Each bristled hair stood like a stake,
When with alarming queer crake crake
        I saw you spring
Away you flighted like a drake,
        On whistling wing.

Let warlocks grim, and withered hags,
Tell how you, on ragweed nags,
They skim o'er moors and dizzy crags,
        In speedy droves,
And in churchyards renew their leagues,
        O'er open graves.

The country wives, with toil and pain,
May plunge and plunge the churn in vain.
The yellow butter it has gone,
        By witching skill,
Their bounteous cows, they too have gone
        As dry's a bull.

When thaws dissolve the snowy hoard,
And float the crushing icy board,
Then water-witches haunt the ford,
        By your direction,
And lonely travellers are allured,
        To their destruction.

And oft your moss-traversing lackies
Decoy the wight that late and drunk is;
The bleezing, cursed, mischievous monkeys
        Delude his eyes,
Till in some miry slough he sunk is,
        No more to rise.

When mason's mystic word and grip
In storms and tempests raise you up,
Some cock or cat your rage will stop,
        Or, strange to tell,
The youngest brother you will whip
        Off straight to hell.

Long since in Eden's happy scene,
When youthful Adam's days were green,
And Eve was like my bonnie Jean,
        My dear sweetheart,
A dancing, sweet, young handsome quean,
        With guileless heart.

Then you, you old and stealthy dog,
You came to Paradise incog.,
And gave to man an awful shock,
        (Black be your fall)
And made the infant world to rock,
        And ruined all.

That day you came as in a race,
Your smoky clothes reeked all the place.
You did present your dirty face,
        To finer folk,
And played upon the man of Uz                    +
        Your spiteful jokes.

And how you got him in your thrall,
Depriving him of house and hall,
While boils and blotches did him gall,
        With bitter claw;
But a doubting, tempting wife withal,
        The worst of all.

But all your doings to rehearse,
Your wily snares and fights so fierce,
Since that day Michael did you pierce,          *See Milton*
          Down to this time,          *Paradise Lost' book vl*
Would confuse a Lowland tongue or Erse,
          In prose or rhyme.

And now, old Devil, I know your thinking.
A certain bard, whose ranting, drinking,
Some luckless hour will see him sinking,
          To your black pit;
But faith, he'll turn the corner dodging,
          And cheat you yet.

But fare you well, Old Nick, and so
Just give a thought to sons of woe.
You might perhaps – I do not know –
          Still have a stake –
'Mong men whose lot in life's a blow,
          Even for your sake.

    +    Book of Job 27 10.

## RANTIN' ROVIN' ROBIN

This song is based on events said to have happened at the birth of the poet, when a portion of the cottage was blown in.

There was a lad was born in Kyle,
But what a day and what a style.
I doubt it's hardly worth the while,
To be so nice with Robin.

Our Monarchs hindmost year but one                    *1759.*
Was five and twenty days begun
When a blast of January wind
Gave us the gift of Robin.

The midwife read his tiny hand,
Forecast a life both bold and bland:
This chosen child throughout the land,
Should have the name of Robin.

He'll have misfortune great and small,
But have a heart above them all;
He'll be a credit to us all.
We'll all be proud of Robin.

But sure as three times three make nine,
I see by every score and line
This chap will like the human kind.
I'm proud to know you Robin.

'Good faith', quoth she, 'no doubt you will
Have bonnie lasses more than your fill,
But all your faults will do no ill.
My blessings on you, Robin.'

## SHE SAYS SHE LOVES ME BEST OF A'

So flaxen were her ringlets,
Eyebrows of darker hue,
Bewitchingly o'arching
Two eyes of bonnie blue.
Her smiling, so wiling,
A wretch could ne'er forego:
What pleasure, what treasure,
Those rosy lips do show.
Besides my Chloris' bonnie face
All other faces pall,
And this, my Chloris' dearest charm,
She loves me best of all.

Like harmony in motion
Her ankle is a spy,
Betraying fair proportion;
A saint could not go by.
So warming, so charming,
Her faultless form and air;
Each feature – old nature
Could never do no more.
Hers are the willing chains of love,
By conquering beauty's sovereign law;
And this my Chloris' dearest charm,
She loves me best of all.

Let others love the city,
And gaudy shows at noon.
Give me the lonely valley,
The eve, and rising moon.
Her beaming and gleaming,
Will light our way along,
While falling, recalling,
The thrush concludes his song.
There, my Chloris, wilt thou rove,
By stream and waterfall,
Hearing my vows of truth and love
Echo, 'I love you best of all'.

## HAPPY FRIENDSHIP
### (A drinking song)

Here around the ingle bleezing,
Who's so happy, who's so free?
Though the northern winds blow freezing,
Friendship warms both you and me.

> Happy we are all together,
> Happy are we one and all.
> Time shall see us all a-blether,
> Before we rise and toddle home.

See the miser o'er his treasure,
Gloating with a greedy eye.
Can he feel the glow of pleasure,
Good ale gives to you and I?

Can the peer in silk and ermine
Call his conscience all his own?
His clothes are spun and edged with vermin,
Though he stands before a throne.

Thus then let us all be tossing
Off our pints of foaming beer,
And while around the board they're passing,
Give a toast to all men here.

Friendship makes us all more happy.
Friendship gives us all delight.
Friendship makes us warm and merry.
Friendship brings us here tonight.

## THE CARLE OF KELLYBURN BRAES
### (The old man of Kellyburn hills)

There lived an old man of Kellyburn braes,
And the wife whom he had was the plague of his days.
While walking one day and taking the air,
He met with the Devil abroad from his lair.

Old man: 'I've got a bad wife, sir, that's my complaint,
      For, saving your presence, to her you're a saint.'
Devil:   'It's neither your ox, or your horse that I crave.
      Just give me your wife, I'll make her behave.'

      'Oh welcome most kindly,' the old man said,
      'If you think you can tame her, don't be misled.'
      The Devil he then got the wife on his back,
      Just as a poor pedlar carries his pack.

      He carried her down to his brimstone door,
      Then gave her a push; the jade, how she swore.
      Then first he tells fifty, the pick of his band,
      To guard her severely, but beware of her hand.

      The wife she went through them, just like a
          wild boar.
      Who'er she got hands on, came back for no more.
      Then one of the guards let out a loud hail,
      'Oh help, master, help, or she'll ruin us all.'

      The Devil he swore to see all the strife,
      But pitied the man who was wed to this wife.
      Then he thanked the Lord, the angels as well,
      He was not in wedlock, but safely in Hell.

      Then Satan he travelled again with his pack,
      And to the old man his wife carried back;
      'I've been a devil for all of my life,
      But never knew Hell till I met your wife.'

# LAMENT FOR MARY QUEEN OF SCOTS
## On the approach of spring

Now nature hangs her mantle green
On every blooming tree,
And spreads her sheets of daisies white
Out o'er the grassy lea:
Now Phoebus cheers the crystal streams,
And glads the azure skies;
But nought can glad the weary wight
Who fast in durance lies.


Now skylarks wake the merry morn,
Aloft on dewy wings;
The blackbird in his noontime bower
Makes woodland echoes ring;
The thrush so wild, with many a note,
Sings drowsy day to rest:
In love and freedom they rejoice,
With care nor thrall oppressed.


Now blooms the lily by the bank,
Primroses make their show;
The hawthorn's budding in the glen,
And milk white is the sloe:
The meanest man in fair Scotland
May roam the hills among;
But I, the Queen of all Scotland,
Must lie in prison strong.


I was the Queen of bonnie France,
Where happy I had been;
Where lightly rose I in the morn,
And blythe lay down at e'en.
And I'm the sovereign of Scotland,
And many a traitor's there;
Yet here I lie in foreign band,
And never-ending care.

But as for thee, false woman,
My sister and my foe,           *Queen Eliz. I.*
Grim vengeance yet shall whet the sword
That through thy soul shall go:
The weeping blood in woman's breast
Was never known to thee;
Nor the balm that drops on wounds of woe
From woman's pitying ee.           *eye.*

My son, my son, may kinder stars           *James.*
Upon thy fortunate shine;
And may those pleasures gild thy reign
That ne'er would blink on mine.
God keep thee from thy mother's foes,
Or turn their hearts to thee:
And when thou meets thy mother's friend,
Remember him for me.

O soon to me, may summer-suns
No more light up the morn;
No more, to me, the autumn winds
Wave o'er the yellow corn.
And in the narrow house of death
Let winter round me rave;
And the next flowers that deck the spring
Bloom on my peaceful grave.

## THE RIGS OF BARLEY

There were two Annies who disputed who was the subject of this song. It is not known whether the dispute was about which Annie it was, or about which Annie it was not.

It was upon an August night,
When cornfields are bonnie;
Beneath the moon's unclouded light
I courted my sweet Annie:
The time flew by with careless heed,
Till 'tween the late and early,
With small persuasion, she agreed
To saunter through the barley.

The sky was blue, the wind was still,
The moon was shining clearly:
We both sat down with right good will
In that field of barley:
I knew her heart was all my own,
I loved her most sincerely;
I kissed her over and over again
In that field of barley.

I locked her in my fond embrace,
Her heart was beating rarely:
My blessings on that happy place,
In that field of barley.
And by the moon and stars so bright
That shone that hour so clearly,
She'll always bless that happy night
In that field of barley.

I have been blythe with comrades bold,
I have been merry drinking;
I have been joyful gathering gold,
I have been happy thinking.
But all the pleasures e'er I saw,
Though three times doubled fairly,
That happy night was worth them all
In that field of barley.

## ADDRESS OF BEELZEBUB
(Beelzebub – Prince of darkness. Matthew xii. 24.)


In 1786 five hundred dissatisfied Highlanders prepared to emigrate to Canada 'in search of liberty'. Their masters,to whom they were bound, sought to frustrate them.


Long life, my lord, and health be yours,
Unscathed by hungry Highland boors.
Lord, grant no ragged desperate beggar,
With dirk, claymore, or rusty trigger,
May take from Scotland of a life
She likes – as lambkins like a knife.


Faith, you and Applecross were right
To keep the Highland hounds in sight.
I doubt not they would be no better
Than let them once out o'er the water;
Then up among the lakes and trees
They'll make what rules and laws they please;
Some daring Hancock, or a Franklin,
May set their Highland blood a-tingling;
Some Washington again may head them,
Till God knows what will be effected
When by such heads and hearts directed –
Poor dunghill sons of dirt and mire
May to patrician rights aspire.
No wise old North or wiser Sackville
To watch and premier o'er the pack vile,
Where would you get you Howes and Clintons
To bring them to a right repentence,
To cow the rebel generation,
And save the honour of the nation?
Let them be damned, what right have they
To meat or sleep or light of day?
Far less to riches, power or freedom,
But what your lordship likes to give them.

But hear, my Lord, Glengarry hear,
Your hand's o'er light on them I fear.
Your factors, grieves, trustees and bailies,                    *Stewards.*
I will say this, they do right fairly;
They lay aside all tender mercies,
And take their pound of flesh,
And though they strip them to the hide,
They'll keep their proud and stubborn pride,
But crush them as you would a snail,
And let the debtors rot in jail;
The young dogs? Fling them to their labour,
Let work and hunger make them sober.
The girls? If some of them are pretty,
Consign them all to London city.

And if the wives with dirty spoor
Come begging at your gate and door,
Fluttering in rags alive with fleas,
That frighten all your ducks and geese,
Get out a horse-whip or a fowler,                    *Gun.*
The longest thong – the loudest growler,
And make the tattered gypsies pack
With all their bastards on their back.

Go on my lord, I long to meet you,
And in my house at home to greet you;
With common lords you shall not mingle,
But sit with me beside the ingle;
At my right hand assigned the seat
'Tween Herod's hip and Polycrate, –
Or, if your ingle seat brings sorrow,
Between Almargro and Pizarro;
A seat I'm sure your well deserving;
And till you come – Your humble servant,

June 1st. Anno Mundi 5790 (AD 1786)

## THE POET'S WELCOME
## TO HIS ILLEGITIMATE CHILD

The child was born to a servant of the household while Burns was still a single man. It was accepted and reared by his widowed mother.

Thou'rt welcome child, though mischance got thee.
If ought of thee, or of your mammy,
Shall ever daunt me, or awe me,
    My sweet wee lady,
Or if I blush when you shall call me,
    Sir or Daddy,

Wee image of my bonny Bettie,
I fatherly will kiss and hold thee,
As dear and near my heart I set thee,
    With all good will,
As if the priests had seen me get thee,
    That's out of Hell.

What though they call me fornicator,
And name my name in idle chatter?
The more they talk, I'm known the better,
    So let them rant.
An old wife's tongue's of little matter,
    And full of cant.

Sweet fruit of those the world defy,
My wayward ways have now gone by
Since you came into the world awry,
    With such a fuss.
You'll share my gold if I should die,
    You're one of us.

Though I should be but poorly fed,
You'll be as fine and warmly clad
In thy young years, and nicely bred
    With education,
As any brat of wedlock's bed,
    In all thy station.

And if you be as I would have thee,
Just take the counsel I shall give thee.
A loving father I'll be to thee,
      If thou be spared:
Through all thy childhood years I'll keep thee;
      You'll be well reared.

God grant that you in time inherit
Thy mother's person, grace and merit;
And thy poor worthless Daddy's spirit,
      Without his failings.
'Twill please me more to hear and see it,
      Than thriving mailins.                    *Farms.*

## THE WINTER OF LIFE

A sad plaintive song, composed when depressed.

But lately seen in gladsome green,
The woods rejoiced the day,
Through gentle showers the laughing flowers
In double pride were gay.
But now the joys are fled
On wintry winds away.
Oh maiden May, in rich array,
Will I see you again?

From my white head no gentle thaw,
Can melt the snow of age.
My trunk is old, by nature's law,
Is bent by winter's rage.
Oh age has weary days,
And nights of sleepless pain.
The golden time of youthful prime,
Why come ye not again?

## GREEN GROW THE RASHES

There's nought but care on every hand,
In every hour that passes,
But what sustains the life of man?
'Tis the life that's in the lasses.

      Green grow the rushes O,
      Green grow the rushes O.
      The sweetest hours that e'er I spent,
      Were spent among the lasses O.

The worldly race may riches chase,
They struggle sore to find them,
And though at last they catch them fast,
Their hearts can ne'er enjoy them.

Give me a happy hour at e'en,
With my arms about my dear,
And worldly men with harrassed mien
To fulfulment ne'er come near.

Oh you so sour, who sneer at this,
You're nought but senseless asses.
The wisest man the world e'er saw,
He dearly loved the lasses.

Old Nature swears the lovely dears,
Her noblest work she classes,
Her 'Prentice hands he tried on man,
And then she made the lasses.

## Mary Campbell

The following poems/songs are to Mary Campbell with whom Burns was enamoured at the time he was contemplating emigrating to the West Indies. They plighted their troths and exchanged Bibles. Sadly, Mary died suddenly of a fever.

Biographers are in some confusion over the episode and the chronology of the poems/songs. Certain it is that 'Mary in Heaven' was composed three years after her death, when Burns was then married.

### MARY

Powers celestial, whose protection,
Ever guards the virtuous fair,
While in distant climes I wander,
Let my Mary be your care;
Let her form so fair and faultless,
Fair and faultless as your own,
Let my Mary's kindred spirit
Draw your choicest influence down.

Make the gales that waft around her
Soft and pleasing as her breast;
Breathing in the breeze that fans her,
Sooth her bosom into rest.
Guardian angel, O protect her,
When in distant lands I roam,
To realms unknown where fate exiles me,
Make her bosom still my home.

## WILL YE GO TO THE INDIES, MY MARY?

Will ye go to the Indies, my Mary?
And leave old Scotland's shore?
Will ye go to the Indies, my Mary?
Across the Atlantic's roar?

O sweet grow the lime and the orange,
And the cones upon the pine,
But all the charm of the Indies
Can never equal thine.

I ha'e sworn by the heavens to my Mary,
O ha'e sworn by the heavens to be true,
And so may the heavens forget me
When I forget my vow.

O plight me your faith, my Mary,
And plight me your lily white hand;
O plight me your faith, my Mary,
Before I leave Scotland's land.

We have plighted our troth, my Mary,
In mutual affection to join,
And cursed be the cause that shall part us,
The hour and moment of time.

## HIGHLAND MARY

Ye banks and braes and streams around
The castle of Montgomery,
Green be your woods, and fair your flowers,
Your waters never dirty.
There summer first unfolds her robes,
And there the longest tarry,
For there I took the last farewell,
Of my sweet Highland Mary.

How sweetly bloomed the gay green birch,
How rich the hawthorn's blossom,
As underneath their fragrant shade
I clasped her to my bosom.
The golden hours, on angel wings,
Flew o'er me and my dearie;
For dear to me as light and life
Was my sweet Highland Mary.

With many a vow and locked embrace
Our parting was full tender,
And, pledging oft to meet again,
We tore ourselves asunder.
But oh, fell Death's untimely frost,
That nipped my flower so early.
Now green's the sod, and cold's the clay
That wraps my Highland Mary.

O pale, pale now, those rosy lips
I oft have kissed so fondly,
And closed for ever the sparkling glance
That dwelt on me so kindly;
And mouldering now in silent dust
The heart that loved me dearly;
But still within my bosom's core
Shall live my Highland Mary.

## TO MARY IN HEAVEN

Thou lingering star, with lessening ray,
That loved to greet the early morn,
Again thou ushers in the day,
My Mary from my soul was torn.
O Mary, dear departed shade,
Where is thy place of blissful rest?
See'st thy lover lowly laid?
Hear thou the groans that rend his breast?

That sacred hour can I forget?
Can I forget the hallowed grove
Where, by the winding Ayr we met,
To live one day of parting love?
Eternity will not efface
Those records dear of transports past.
Thy image at our last embrace –
Ah, little thought we 'twas our last.

Ayr, gurgling, kissed his pebbled shore,
O'erhung with wild woods, thickening green;
The fragrant birch, and hawthorn hoar,
Twined amorous round the raptured scene.
The flowers sprang wanton to be pressed,
The birds sang love on every spray,
Till, too too soon the glowing west
Proclaimed the speed of wingéd day.

Still o'er these scenes the memory wakes,
And fondly broods with miser care;
Time but the impression stronger makes,
As streams their channel deeper wear.
My Mary, dear departed shade,
Where is thy place of blissful rest?
See'st thou thy lover lowly laid?
Hear thou the groans that rend his breast?

## LINES ON MEETING WITH LORD DAER

Burns had been invited out to dinner and by chance Lord
Daer also attended. The poet was agreeably surprised at his
charm and modesty.

This to all whom it concerns,
I, Rhymer Robbie, alias Burns,
     October twenty-third,
A ne'er to be forgotten day,
When I sauntered up the way,
     And had dinner with a lord.

I've been at drunken lawyers' feasts,
Have been dead drunk 'mong godly priests,
     (With reverence be it spoken);
I've even poured out jugs of ale
Where squires drunk it by the pail,
     Their hydra thirst to slake.

But with a lord – to dine with him,
The son of a peer of the realm,
     Up higher yet my bonnet.
And such a lord – full six feet tall,
He overlooks the peerage all,
     As I look o'er my sonnet.

But, O for Hogarth's magic power,
To show the poet's bewildered glower,
     And how he stared and stammered,
While reeling forward his Grace to meet
And, stumbling on his ploughman's feet,
     He in the parlour lumbered.

I, sidling, sheltered in a nook
And at his lordship stole a look,
     Like some portentous omen;
Except good sense and social glee,
And, what surprised me modesty,
     I markéd nought uncommon.

I watched the symptoms of the great –
The gentle grace, the lordly state,
    No arrogance assuming,
I looked for pride, no pride had he,
But complete compatibility,
    Just like an honest ploughman.

Then from his lordship I shall learn,
Henceforth to meet with unconcern
    One rank as well's another;
No honest worthy man need care
To meet the noble, youthful Daer,
    For he but meets a brother.

## BONNIE JEAN

There was a lass and she was fair,
At church or market to be seen.
When all the fairest maids were met,
The fairest one was bonnie Jean.

She always wrought her daily work,
And always sang so merrily.
The blithest bird upon the bush
Had ne'er a lighter heart than she.

But hawks will rob the tender joys,
That bless the linnet's nest,
And frost will blight the fairest flowers,
And love will break the soundest rest.

Young Robin was the finest lad,
The flower and pride of all the glen,
And he had oxen, sheep and kye,
And wanton horses nine or ten.

He went with Jeanie to the tryst,
He danced with Jeanie on the down,
And long ere witless Jeanie wist,
Her heart was lost, her peace was gone.

As in the bosom of the stream
The moonbeam dwells at dewy e'en,
So, trembling, pure was tender love,
Within the breast of bonnie Jean.

And now she plies her daily work,
And now she sighs with care and pain.
She does not know what ails her so,
But wants young Robin back again.

But did not Jeanie's heart leap light,
And did not joy blink in her eye,
As Robin told a tale of love,
Beneath the star-filled sky?

Oh Jeanie fair, I love thee dear.
Oh can you think to fancy me,
And will you leave your mother's home,
And learn to tend the farm with me?

In barn or byre you shall not drudge,
Nothing more will trouble thee;
But stray among the heather bells,
And view the waving corn with me.

Now what could artless Jeanie do?
She had no will or thoughts of rue.
At length she blushed a sweet consent,
And love was e'er between those two.

## YE HA'E LIEN WRANG, LASSIE

You have lain wrong lassie,
You have lain wrong,
You've lain too long in a stranger's bed,
And with a stranger man.

Your rosy cheeks have turned so wan,
You're greener than the grass, lassie.
Your coat is shorter by a span,
But you're not an inch the taller, lassie.

Oh lassie, you have played the fool,
And you will feel the scorn, lassie.
You'll feel like one who's broke a rule,
Both wretched and forlorn, lassie.

Oh once you danced so blithe and gay,
And through the woods you sang, lassie;
But now your life is dull and gray,
I'm afraid that you've been stung, lassie.

## WILLIE CHALMERS

'Mr. W. Chalmers, a gentleman in Ayrshire, a particular
friend of mine, asked me to write a poetic epistle to a young
lady, his dulcinea. I had seen her, but was scarcely acquainted
with her, and wrote as follows.' – Burns.

On a fine new saddle I ride in pride,
With fine new reins for guiding.
My fine new mare I sit astride,
And to my love come riding.
While o'er a bush with downward crush
The stupid beastie stammers,
Then up he gets, and off he sets,
For sake of Willie Chalmers.

I doubt not, lass, that well-known name
May cost a pair of blushes;
I am no stranger to your fame,
Nor his warm urgéd wishes.
Your bonnie face, so mild and sweet,
His honest heart enamours.
Reciprocation's no mean feat,
Though spent on Willie Chalmers.

Old Truth herself might swear you fair,
And Honour safely back her,
And Modesty assume your air;
Let not a man mistake her.
And such two love-inspiring eyes,
Might fire the ancient psalmers,
And brought so many heart-felt sighs,
To honest Willie Chalmers.

Though fickle fortune holds the offer
Of a prim and proper priest,
From such a fate you need not suffer,
Though he swears with hand on breast.
For oh, what signifies to you
His lexicons and grammars?
The feeling heart's the royal blue,
And that's with Willie Chalmers.

Some gaping, glowering, country laird
May contemplate your favour,
May pull his ear, and stroke his beard,
And give you his palaver.
My bonnie maid, before you choose
An oaf devoid of manners,
Seek Heaven for help before you lose
A man like Willie Chalmers.

Forgive the bard, my fond regard,
For one who shares my bosom,
Inspires my muse to give him his dues
Of flattery right fulsome.
May powers above unite you soon,
And fructify your amours,
And every year come in more dear,
To you and Willie Chalmers.

## THE BRIGS OF AYR
### (The Bridges of Ayr)

Inscribed to John Ballantine, Esq. of Ayr.

The New Bridge was erected in 1786 when John Ballantine
was mayor. The Old Bridge was erected in about 1500. The
poem is partly allegorical in that the two bridges represent
Age and Modernity, with the inevitable rancour between them.

The simple bard, rough at the rustic plough,
Learning his tuneful trade from every bough –
The chanting linnet, or the mellow thrush,
Hailing the setting sun, sweet, in the green thorn bush;
The soaring lark, the perching red-breast shrill,
Or deep-toned plovers, gray, wild whistling o'er the hill –
Shall he, nursed in the peasants' lowly shed,
To hardy independence bravely bred,
By early poverty to hardship steeled,
And trained to arms in stern misfortune's field –
Shall he be guilty of their hireling crimes,
The servile mercenary Swiss of rhymes?
Or labour hard the panegyric close,
With all the venal soul of dedicating prose?
No; though his artless strains he rudely sings,
And throws his hand uncouthly o'er the strings,
He glows with all the spirit of the bard,
Fame, honest fame, his great, his dear reward.
Still, if some patron's generous care he trace,
Skilled in the secret to bestow with grace;
When Ballantine befriends his humble name,
And hands the rustic stranger up to fame,
With heartfelt throes his grateful bosom swells.
The godlike bliss, to give, alone excels.

'Twas when the stacks are clothed on top,
And thatch and rope secure the crop,
Potato-heaps are covered from all harms,
From frosty winds and such alarms;
The bees, rejoicing o'er their summer toils,
Unnumbered buds and flowers, delicious spoils,

Sealed up with care in massive waxen piles,
Are doomed by man, the tyrant of the weak,
The death of devils smothered with brimstone reek:
The thundering guns are heard on every side,
The wounded coveys, reeling, scatter wide;
The feathered field-mates, bound by Nature's tie,
Sires, mothers, children, in one carnage lie:
(What warm, poetic heart but inward bleeds,
And execrates man's savage, ruthless deeds;)
No more the flower in field or meadow springs;
No more the grove with airy concert rings,
Except perhaps the robin's whistling glee,
Proud of the height of a half-grown tree:
The frosty morn precedes the sunny day,
Mild, calm, serene, wide spreads the noon-tide blaze,
While thick the gossamer waves wanton in the rays.

'Twas in that season when a simple bard,
Unknown and poor, simplicity's reward,
One night, within the ancient town of Ayr,
By whim inspired, or haply pressed with care,
He left his bed, and took his wayward route,
And by the tavern wheeled the left about.
Whether impelled by all-directing fate
To witness what I after shall narrate;
Or whether, rapt in meditation high,
He wandered out, he knew not where or why.
The drowsy Town Hall clock had numbered two,
The Minster echoed it was true:
The tide-swollen firth, with sullen-sounding roar,
Through the still night dashed hoarse along the shore:
All else was hushed, all nature slept,
The silent moon her vigil kept;
The chilly frost, beneath her silver beam,
Crept, gently crusting o'er the glittering stream.

When, lo, on either hand the listening Bard,
The clanging sough of whistling wings is heard;
Two dusky forms dart through the midnight air,
Swift as the hawk drives on the wheeling hare:
One on the Old Bridge his airy shape uprears,

The other flutters o'er the rising piers:
Our warlock Rhymer instantly descry'd
The sprites that o'er Ayr's bridges preside.
(That bards are second-sighted is no joke,
They know the language of the spiritual folk;
Fairies, witches, kelpies, they can explain them,
Even the Devil is well known to them.)
The Old Bridge was of ancient Pictish race,
The very wrinkles Gothic in his face:
He seemed as if with Time he'd striven sore,
Yet firmly made, withstood the river's roar.
New Bridge was fashioned with a coat
That was from London newly brought;
Its tapered piers, smooth as marble,
With whirls and carvings ornamental.
Old Bridge stalked round with anxious search,
Spying for flaws in every arch;
His new-come neighbour, finely wrought,
Kindled in him envious thought.
With spiteful sneer to see such graceful form,
He down the water gave him this good-morn:-

I doubt not friend that you will swank
When once you're stretched from bank to bank,
But when you're a bridge as old as me –
Perhaps that day you'll never see –
But if it comes let it be said,
You'll shed fine notions from your head.

## NEW BRIG

Old vandal, you show but little sense;
Your head, like stone, is very dense;
Will your poor, narrow footpath of a street
Where two wheel barrows tremble when they meet;
Ruined formless bulk of stone and lime,
Compare with a bridge of modern time?
There's men of taste would use the upstream ford,
Would wet their shanks and rust their sword,
Ere they would grate their feelings with the view
Of such an ugly Gothic hulk like you.

## AULD BRIG

Conceited upstart, puffed up with pride,
For many years I've stood the flood and tide;
And though I'm agéd and forlorn,
I'll be a bridge when you're a cairn.
As yet you little apprehend the matter,
But two-three winters will inform you better.
When heavy, dark, continued, all-day rains,
With deepening deluge drown the plains;
When from the hills where springs the brawling Coil,
Or stately Lugar's mossy fountains boil,
Or where the Greenock winds his moorland course,
Or ghostly Garbal draws his feeble source,
Aroused by blustering winds and rapid thaws,
The torrents fed by melting snows;
While crashing ice, borne on the roaring spate,
Gives dams and bridges a watery fate.
From source to sea in foaming flow,
Old Ayr will render blow on blow,
And down you'll tumble, no more to rise,
Submerged and humbled by the pouring skies:
A lesson sadly teaching, to your cost,
That Architecture's noble art is lost.

## NEW BRIG

Fine architecture, on my oath I have this to say of it:
The Lord be thankful we have lost the way of it,
Gaunt, ghastly, ghost-alluring edifices,
Hanging with threatening jut-like precipices;
Over-arching, mouldy, gloom inspiring coves,
Supporting roofs fantastic, stony groves:
Windows and doors, in nameless sculptures dressed,
With order, symmetry, or taste unblessed:
Forms like some demented carver's dream,
The crazed creation of misguided whim;
Forms might be worshipped on the bended knee,
And still the second dread command be free.
Their likeness is not found on earth, in air, or sea.
Mansions that would disgrace the building taste,

Of any mason, reptile, bird, or beast;
Fit only for a dim-wit monkish race,
Or frosty maids who've forsworn the dear embrace;
Or fools of later times, who held the notion
That sullen gloom was sterling true devotion;
Fancies that our fine town denies protection,
And soon they may expire, unblest with resurrection.

## AULD BRIG

O ye, my dear-remembered, ancient friends,
Were ye but here to stop these trends,
Worthy mayors, sons of the soil,
Who in the paths of righteousness did toil;
Ye dainty deacons, and sage convenors,
To whom our moderns are roadway cleaners;
Ye godly councils who have blessed this town;
Ye godly brethren of the sacred gown,
Who meekly turned the cheek to other smiters,
And (what would now be strange) ye lawers.
All ye kind folk I've borne above the Ayr,
What would ye say or do, if ye were here?
How would your spirits groan in deep vexation
To see each melancholy alteration;
And, agonizing, curse the time and place
When ye begat the base, degenerate race.
No longer reverend men, the Country's glory,
In plain broad Scots hold forth a plain broad story;
No longer thrifty citizens, sage and sombre,
Meet o'er a pint, or in a council-chamber;
But half-wit wooden-headed, graceless gentry,
The devastation and ruin of the country;
Men three parts made by tailors and by barbers,
Who waste good gold on surplus bridges?

## NEW BRIG

Now hold it there, you've had your say,
And you have also had your day;
As for the priesthood, I shall say but little,
For crows' and clergy's ways are brittle,

But, under favour of your longer beard,
Abuse of magistrates might well be spared:
To liken them to your old-world squad,
I must needs say, comparisons are odd.
In Ayr, quick-witted wags they have no standing,
To use 'French citizen' a term of scandal
No more the council waddles down the street,
In all the pomp of ignorant conceit;
Men who walked in such processions,
Traded in bonds and re-possessions.
If haply Knowledge, on a random tramp,
Enlightened them with a glimmer of his lamp,
And would to Common-sense for once betrayed them,
Plain, dull Stupidity stepped kindly in to aid them.

When further fraction might have led
To bloody wars, if sprites had any blood to shed,
No man can tell, but all before their sight
A fairy train appeared in order bright;
Adown the glittering stream they spritely pranced;
Bright to the moon their various dresses glanced;
Dancing o'er the watery glass so neat,
The infant ice scarce bent beneath their feet;
The arts of minstrels among them rung,
And soul-uplifting bards heroic ditties sung.
Oh, had M'Lauchline, warm, inspiring sage,          *Local violinist.*
Been here to hear this heavenly band engage,
When through his dear strathspeys they bore with
          Highland rage;
Or when they struck old Scotland's melting airs,
The lover's raptured joys or bleeding cares;
How would his Highland ear been nobly fired,
And even his matchless hand with finer touch inspired?
No guess could tell what instrument appeared,
But all the soul of Music's self was heard;
Harmonious concert rung in every part,
While simple melody poured moving on his heart.

The Genius of the Stream in front appears,
A venerable chief advanced in years;
His hoary head with water-lilies crowned,
His manly leg with garter tangle bound.
Next came the loveliest pair in all the ring,
Sweet Female Beauty hand in hand with Spring;
Then, crowned with flowery hay, came Rural Joy,
And Summer, with his fervid-beaming eye:
All-cheering Plenty, with her flowing horn,
Led yellow Autumn wreathed with nodding corn;
The Winter's time-bleached locks did hoary show,
By Hospitality with cloudless brow.
Next followed Courage with his martial stride,
From where the Feal wild woody coverts hide;
Benevolence, with mild, benignant air,
A female form, came from the towers of Stair;     *Mrs Stewart of*
Learning and Worth in equal measures trode,            *Stair House.*
From simple Catrine, their long-loved abode;
Last, white-robed Peace, crowned with hazel wreath,
To rustic Agriculture did bequeath
The broken iron instruments of death,–
At sight of whom our sprites forgot their kindling wrath.

## A DEDICATION TO GAVIN HAMILTON ESQ.

Gavin Hamilton was a legal practitioner and a man of good standing in Mauchline. He was a friend and patron of Burns. Allies in parochial matters, both had received strictures from the Church, to which Burns alludes in several of his poems.

Expect not sir, in this narration
A flattering, fawning, dedication
To rouse you up and call you good,
And sprung from great and noble blood,
Because you're surnamed like his Grace –     *Duke of Hamilton.*
Perhaps related to the race;
Then when I'm tired and so are ye,
With many a fulsome, sinful lie,
Set up a face, how I stop short,
For fear your modesty be hurt.

This may do-must do, sir, with them who
Must please the great folk with a thankyou;
For me, so low, I need not bow,
For, Lord be thankful, I can plough:
And when I cannot yoke a nag,
Then Lord be thankful, I can beg;
So I shall say, and that's no flattering,
No poet had a better patron.

The poet, some good angel help him,
Lest his critics combine to belt him.
He may do well for all he's done yet,
The danger is what he will do next.

The patron, (sir, you must forgive me;
I will not lie, come what will to me)
On every hand I will allowed be,
He's just-no better than he should be.

I readily and freely grant
He cannot see a poor man want;
What's not his own he will not take it,
What once he says he will not break it.

Ought he can lend he'll not refuse it,
Although his goodness is abuséd;
The rascal who will do him wrong,
Even that, he does not mind it long;
As master, landlord, husband, father,
He does not fail his part in either.


But then, no thanks to him for all that;
No godly symptom he can call that;
It's nothing but a milder feature
Of our poor sinful, corrupt nature.
You'll get the best of moral works
Among black Gentoos and pagan Turks,
Or hunters wild on Ponotaxi
Who never heard of orthodoxy.
That he's the poor man's friend in need,
The gentleman in word and deed,
It's just a worthy inclination.


Morality, thou deadly bane,
Tens of thousands thou hast slain.
Vain is his hope whose stay and trust is,
In moral mercy, truth and justice.


No – stretch a point when proof is lack,
Abuse a brother to his back,
Steal through a window to a whore,
Decry the men who use the door.
Be to the poor like any whinstone,                    *Granite.*
And hold their noses to the grindstone;
Ply every art of legal stealing,
No matter – stick to sound believing.


Learn three mile prayers, and half mile graces,
With well-spread palms, and long wry faces;
Grant up a solemn lengthened groan,
And damn all parties but your own.
I'll warrant then you're no decíever –
A steady, sturdy, staunch believer.

O ye who leave the springs of Calvin
For grubby ponds of your own delving,
Ye sons of heresy and error,
Ye'll some day squeal in quaking terror,
When Vengeance draws the sword of wrath,
And in the fire throws the sheath;
When Ruin, with his sweeping broom,
Just frets till Heaven commission give him;
While o'er the harp pale misery moans,
And strikes the ever deepening tones,
Still louder shrieks, and heavier groans.

Your pardon sir, for this digression –
I almost forgot my dedication;
But when divinity comes across me,
My readers still are sure to lose me.

So, sir, you see 'twas no daft vapour,
But I maturely thought it proper,
When all my works I did review,
To dedicate them, sir, to you:
Because – you need not take it ill –
I thought them something like yoursel'

Then patronize them with your favour,
And your petitioner shall ever –
I had almost said, ever pray,
But that's a word I need not say;
For praying I have but little skill,
And would much rather use my quill;
But I'll repeat each poor man's prayer,
That knows or hears about you, sir.

May ne'er misfortune shade your dwelling,
Or ought to mar your gracious living.
May ne'er his generous, honest heart
For that same generous spirit smart;
May his wife's illustrious name
Long beat his hymeneal flame.
Till Hamiltons, at least a dozen,
Are from their nuptial labours risen;

Five bonnie lasses round their table,
And seven fine fellows, stout and able
To serve their king and country weel,
By word, or pen, or pointed steel.
May health and peace, with mutual rays,
Shine on the evening of his days;
May his grandsons to manhood grow,
When ebbing life no more shall flow,
The last, sad, mournful rites bestow.

I will not wind a long conclusion,
With complimentary effusion;
But whilst your wishes and endeavors
Are blest with Fortune's smiles and favours,
I am, dear sir, with zeal most fervant,
Your much indebted, humble servant.

But if (which Powers above prevent)
That iron-hearted evil, Want,
Attended in his grim advances,
By sad mistakes, and black mischances,
While hopes, and joys, and pleasures fly him,
Make you as poor a dog as I am –
Your humble servant then no more;
For who would humbly serve the poor?
But, by a poor man's hopes in heaven,
While recollection's power is given,
If, in the vale of humble life,
The victim sad of Fortune's strife,
I, through the tender gushing tear,
Should recognise my master dear;
If friendless, low, we meet together,
Then, sir, your hand – my friend and brother.

# NOTHING

This poem was not discovered and published until 70 years after Burns' death. It was addressed to his friend Gavin Hamilton.

To you, Sir, this summons I've sent,
Take heed to all that I'm saying;
But if you should ask what I want,
I honestly answer you – nothing.

Ne'er scorn a poor poet like me,
For idly living and breathing;
While people of every degree
Are busy employed doing – nothing.

The miserable miser may fast,
And deny his body of clothing;
He'll find when the balance is cast,
He's gone to the Devil for – nothing.

A courtier cringes and bows,
Ambition has likewise its plaything;
A coronet beams on his brows,
And what is a coronet? – nothing.

Quarrels 'mongst clergy have grown,
Quarrels about everything;
But every good fellow will own
The quarrels are all about – nothing.

The lover may sparkle and glow,
Approaching his bonnie bright thing;
But marriage will soon let him know,
He's dressed himself up for – nothing.

The poet may jingle and rhyme,
In hopes of a laureate wreathing;
But when he has wasted his time,
He's kindly rewarded with – nothing.

The thundering bully may rage,
And swagger and swear like a heathen;
But collar him fast and I'll wage
You'll find that his courage is – nothing.

Last night with a feminine prude,
(Poets she never had faith in)
But whether she should'nt or should,
I showed her her fears came to – nothing.

The prude was pleasantly pleased,
And charmingly tickled with one thing;
Her fingers I lovingly squeezed,
I kissed her and promised her – nothing.

Postulating priests have been known,
To confuse the state that we're all in;
But when Honour's reveille is blown
The holy artillery is – nothing.

And now I must mount on the wave,
My voyage perhaps there is death in;
But what of a watery grave?
A drowning poor poet is – nothing.

And now as grim death's in my thought
To you, Sir, I make this bequeathing;
My service as long as you've aught,
And my friendship, my God, when you've – nothing.

## O LASSIE ART THOU SLEEPING YET

O lassie art thou sleeping yet,
Or are you waiting and awake?
For love of you I nightly fret,
Please let me in for my own sake.

> O let me in this very night,
> This very night, this very night,
> For pity's sake this very night,
> Arise and let me in.

No stars blink down through driving sleet,
The wintry winds made me entreat,
Take pity on my weary feet,
And shield me from the rain.

The bitter blast that round me blows,
Unheeded howls, unheeded woes,
The coldness of your heart's the cause,
Of all my grief and pain.

Her reply:
O tell not me of wind and rain,
Upbraid not me with cold disdain,
Go back the way you came again.
I will not let you in.

> I tell you once this very night,
> This very night, this very night,
> And once for all this very night,
> I will not let you in.

The coldest blast at darkest hour,
That round the pathless wanderer pours,
Is nought to what poor me endures
Who trusted faithless man.

The sweetest flower that decked the mead,
Now trodden like the vilest weed.
Let simple maid the lesson read,
That fate might be her own.

The bird that charmed the summer day,
Is now the cruél fowler's prey.
Let witless, trusting women say
How oft her fate's the same.

## OH, MALLY'S MEEK, MALLY'S SWEET

## (MARY'S MEEK, MARY'S SWEET)

As I meandered down the street,
A barefoot maid I chanced to meet,
But oh the road was very hard,
For that fair maiden's tender feet.

Mary's meek, Mary's sweet,
Mary's modest and discreet,
Mary's rare, Mary's fair,
Mary's everyway complete.

It was more meet, that those fine feet,
Were placed in silken hose,
And 'twere more fit, that she should sit,
On any throne she chose.

Her yellow hair, beyond compare,
Comes trickling down her swan-like neck;
And her two eyes, like stars in skies,
Would keep a sinking ship from wreck.

## A BARD'S EPITAPH

This is surely the most succinct of autobiographies. Written by Burns in his twenty-eighth year, Wordsworth paid a handsome tribute to it for its sincerity, prophecy and foreboding.

Is there a whim – inspiréd fool,
Too fast for thought, too hot to rule,
Too shy to seek, too proud to fawn?
     Let him draw near;
And o'er this plot of heaving lawn,
      Shed just one tear.

Is there a bard of rustic song,
Who, noteless, steals the crowds among,
That weekly this area throng?
     O, pass not by;
But, with a brother feeling strong,
      Here give a sigh.

Is there a man whose judgement clear,
Can others teach the course to steer,
Yet runs, himself, life's mad career,
     Wild as the wave?
Here pause – and, through the starting tear,
      Survey this grave.

The poor inhabitant below
Was quick to learn, and wise to know,
And keenly felt the kindly glow,
     And softer flame;
But thoughtless follies laid him low,
      And stained his name.

Reader attend – whether thy soul
Soars fancy's flights beyond the pole,
Or darkling grubs this earthly hole,
     In low pursuit;
Know, prudent, cautious self control
      Is wisdom's root.

## OH, WILLIE BREWED A PECK OF MALT

Oh, Willie brewed a peck of malt,
Which Rab and Allen tasted.
Those three blythe hearts could find no fault,
Ensured that none was wasted.

We are not drunk but sober men,
Old friendships we'll renew,
The cock may crow, the day may dawn,
But still we'll sup Will's barley brew,

Here are we met, three merry boys,
Three merry boys I vow we are,
And many a night we've merry been,
And many more we hope to be.

It is the moon, the lovers' mate,
That's shining in the sky.
She'll have to wait, although it's late,
Till we've drunk Willie dry.

Who first shall rise to go away,
A cuckold coward loon is he,
Who last beside his chair can sway,
He is the king among us three.

## THE POSIE

Oh love will venture in where it dare not well be seen,
Oh love will venture in where wisdom once has been,
But I will down that river rove, among the woods so green,
And all to pull a posie to my own dear May.

The primrose I will pull, the first one of the year,
And I will pull the pink, the emblem of my dear,
For she's the pink of womankind, and blooms without a peer,
And all to pull a posie to my own dear May.

I'll pull the budding rose when Phoebus peeps in view,
It's like the balmy kiss of the sweet honey-dew,
And the hyacinth for constancy with its unchanging blue,
And all to pull a posie to my own dear May.

The lily it is pure, the lily it is fair,
And in her lovely bosom, I'll place the lily there,
The daisy for simplicity and unaffected air,
And all to pull a posie to my own dear May.

The hawthorn I will pull, with its locks of silver grey,
Where, like an aged man, it stands at break of day,
But the songbird's nest within the bush I will not take away,
And all to pull a posie to my own dear May.

The woodbine I will pull, when the evening star is near,
And the diamond drops of dew shall be her eyes so clear,
The violet for modesty, which she will always wear,
And all to pull a posie for my own dear May.

I'll tie the posie round with the silken band of love,
I'll place it on her breast, and I'll swear by all above
That till my latest draught of life, the band we'll ne'er remove,
And this will be a posie to my own dear May.

## ANSWER TO A POETICAL EPISTLE

Thomas Walker, a tailor, had the temerity to write a poem to Burns criticising him on his conduct, one verse ran thus:-

Oh Rab lay by your foolish tricks,
Molest no more the fairer sex,
For if you treat them so uncivil,
You'll find no comfort with the devil.

Burns replied;

What ails you now, you lousy beggar,
To knife me in the back?
May God show mercy to you, Walker,
    So spare me from the wrack.
More mercy ministers have shown me,
    In their strictures black.

What though at times I do carouse,
And give the dames their needs;
No need to let your spleen arouse
    To tell me where it leads.
Just mind your stitches and your seams,
    And spare me such long reams.

King David of poetic brief          *2nd Samuel 5–13.*
Wrought 'mong the lasses such mischief,
That filled his after life with grief,
    And bloody rants,
And yet he's ranked among the chief
    Of old time saints.

And, maybe Tam, for all my faults,
My wicked rhymes, and drunken pranks,
I'll give the Devil and his haunts,
    A clever slip,
And snugly sit among the saints,
    At David's hip.

But faith, the Session says I must                                    *Church.*
Not look on lasses with such lust,
Nor turn them topsy turvy,
  But keep them all from bearing
The sorely suffering mother's looks
  At their daughter's failing.

This leads me on to tell for sport
Confusion with the Session wrought.
The sidesman was a sour sort
  Cried three times – Robin;
Come hither, lad, for now you're caught,
  By girls that you've been robbin'.

At this I put my Sunday face on,
And humbly sat before the Session.
I made an open fair confession –
  I scorned to lie,
And then an Elder with fierce expression,
  Fell foul of me.

A fornicator lout he called me,
And said my faults from bliss expelled me;
I own the tale was true he told me,
  But what the matter?
Quoth I, 'I fear unless you geld me
  I'll not be better.'

'Geld you,' quoth he, 'suppose it's so
If your right hand, leg, or toe
Should ever prove your spiritual foe,
  You should remember
To cut them off, extend this to
  Your dearest member.'

'No, no,' quoth I, 'I'm not for that,
Gelding's no better than all this cant
I'd rather suffer for my fault
  A hearty beating,
And let you give a jarring jolt,
  To my seating.'

'Or, if you like to end this fuss,
To please us all may I suggest,
That when next time I'm with a lass
        I'll lie beside her;
And if anything should come to pass,
        She'll be the guider.'

But, sir, this pleased them worst of all,
And therefore Tam, before them all
I said 'goodnight' to one and all,
        And left the Session,
I saw they were resolvéd all,
        On my oppression.

## TRAVELLING TINKER'S SONG

O merry I've been working with metal,
And merry I've been shaping a spoon,
Merry I've been mending a kettle,
And kissing my Katie when it was all done.
Working all day from dawn until late,
All the long day I whistle and sing,
And all the long night I cuddle my Kate,
And all the long night I'm happy's a king.

But I married Bess to get better winnings,          *Dowry.*
I married Bess and became but a slave:
Blest be the day she cooled in her linens,          *Shroud.*
And blithe be the bird that sings on her grave.
Come to my arms, my Katie, my Katie,
And come to my arms and kiss me again,
Drunken or sober, here's to thee Kate,
And blest be the day I married again.

## THERE WAS A LASS

There was a lass, they called her Meg,
Upon the moors she liked to spin.
There was a lad that followed her,
They called him Duncan Davidson.
He knew not why, the lass was shy,
Her favours Duncan could not win,
For with a rock, she would him knock,
And always took a rolling pin.

As o'er the moor they lightly sped,
The stream was clear, the glen was green,
Upon the banks they eased their shanks,
But always set the wheel between.
Then Duncan swore an oath with zeal,
That Meg would be a bride the morn,
Meg then took her spinning wheel,
And flung it far out o'er the burn.                    *Stream.*

We'll build a house, a wee, wee house,
And we will live like king and queen;
So blithe and merry we will be,
When we sit by the fire at e'en.
A man may drink and not be drunk,
A man may fight and not be slain,
A man may kiss a bonnie lass,
And still be welcome back again.

## THE VISION

This abridged poem finds the author in a despondent mood,
feeling unrewarded and worthless. The timely appearance
of an ethereal 'vision' helps to dispel this.


The sun had closed the winter day,
The curlers quit their roaring play,
And hungry hares made their way,
  To pastures green,
The faithless snows each step betray,
  Where they have been.

The flailers weary work with wheat and rye,
This whole long day's brought many a sigh,
And when the day has closed his eye,
  Far in the west,
To my own hearth, my way I'll hie,
  To seek my rest.

There, lonely by the ingle – cheek,
I'll sit amongst the smoking reek
That floats about in wraith and wreath
  My old clay cottage;
I hear the restless rats give squeak,
  As round they forage.

All in this moist and misty clime,
I backward mused on wasted time,
How I had spent my youthful prime,
  In doing nothing,
But stringing nonsense up in rhyme,
  For fools to sing.

Had I to good advice but taken heed,
I might, by this, be not in need,
Only to saunter to a bank and check
  My cash account,
But here, half mad, half fed, half wreck,
  Is my amount.

I cursed myself, all I could stand,
And held on high my horny hand,
And swore by gods of every land,
    Or some such oath,
Henceforward I'd be free from verse
    Till my last breath.

When click: the string drew latch aside,
And let the door fly open wide,
And by the firelight I espied,
    Now blazing bright,
A maid who would with Helen vied,
    Come full in sight.

You need not doubt I held my peace,
The half formed oath I had to cease.
I felt as though I had been crushed,
    And turned to hide,
When sweet like, modest worth she blushed,
    And stepped inside.

Green, slender, leaf-like holly boughs
Were twisted graceful, round her brows;
I took her for some Scottish muse,
    By that same token,
And come to stop those reckless vows,
    Lest they be broken.

Down flowed her robe of tartan sheen,
Till half a leg was clearly seen,
And such a leg: my bonnie Jean
    Could only match it;
So straight, so tapered, neat and clean,
    None else came near it.

Her mantle large, of greenish blue,
My gazing wonder chiefly drew;
Deep lights and shades of every hue
    Did emanate.
She then implored me not to rue,
    My rueful state.

'All hail, my own inspired bard:
In me thy native muse regard:
Nor longer mourn thy fate is hard.
        Thus poorly low,
I come to give thee such reward
        As we bestow.

To lower orders are assigned
The humbler ranks of humankind –
The rustic bard, the labouring kind,
        The artisan;
All choose, as various they're inclined,
        The various man.

'When youthful love, warm-blushing, strong,
Keen-shivering shot thy nerves along,
Those accents, grateful to thy tongue,
        The adored Name,
I taught thee how to pour in song,
        To soothe thy flame.

'I taught thy manners paining strains,
The loves, the ways, of simple swains,
Till now, o'er all my wide domains
        Thy fame extends,
And some, the pride of Scotland's plains,
        Become thy friends.

'Yet all beneath the unrivalled rose,
The lowly daisy sweetly blows,
Though large the forests's monarch throws
        His grateful shade,
Yet green the juicy hawthorn grows
        Adown the glade.

'Then never murmur or repine;
Strive in thy humble sphere to shine;
And do not trust the Midas touch,
        Nor kings regard.
They cannot give what means so much,
        To a rustic bard.

'To give my counsels all in one,
Thy tuneful flame still careful fan,
Preserve the dignity of man,
        With soul erect;
And trust the Universal plan
        Will all protect.

'And wear this,' – she solemn said,
And bound the holly round my head;
The polished leaves, and berries red,
        Did rustling play;
And, like a passing thought, she fled
        In light away.

## VERSES

On the destruction of picturesque woodland, for mercenary purposes, by the absentee landlord, the Duke of Queensbury

As on the banks of wandering Nith,
One smiling summer morn I strayed,
And traced its bonnie banks and braes,
Where linnets sang and lambkins played,
I sat me down upon a crag,
And drank my fill of fancy's dream,
When from the eddying deep below
Uprose the genius of the stream.

Dark, like the frowning rock, his brow,
And troubled like his wintry wave,
And deep, as soughs the boding wind
Among his caves, the sigh he gave –
'And come you here my son,' he cried,
'To wander in my birches shade?
To muse some favourite Scottish theme,
Or serenade some Scottish maid?

There was a time, not long ago,
You might have seen me in my pride,
When all the banks so bravely saw
Their woody pictures in my tide;
When hanging beech and spreading elm
Shaded my stream so clear and cool;
And stately oaks their twisted arms
Threw broad and dark across the pool.

When, glinting through the trees, appeared,
That little house above the mill,
And peaceful rose its spiral smoke,
That slowly curling climbed the hill.
But now the house is bare and cold,
Its leafy shelter for ever gone,
And scarce a stunted birch is left,
To shiver in the blast alone.'

'Alas,' said I 'what rueful chance,
Has taken all your stately trees,
Has laid your rocky bosom bare,
And stripped the clothing from your screes?
Was it the bitter eastern blast,
That scatters blight in early spring,
Or did some fire scorch the boughs,
Or canker-worm with secret sting?'

'No eastern blast,' the sprite replied;
'It blows not here so fierce and fell,
And on my dry and wholesome banks
No canker-worm gets leave to dwell:
Man, cruel man,' the genius sighed –
As through the cliffs he sank him down –
'The worm that gnawed my bonnie trees,
That reptile– wears a ducal crown.'

## THE EPISTLES TO JOHN LAPRAIK

This was the song, by John Lapraik, that so entranced Burns that he determined to acquaint himself with the author:-

When I upon thy bosom lean,
And fondly hold thee all my own,
I glory in the sacred ties,
That made us one when we were twain.
A mutual flame inspired us both –
The tender look, the melting kiss;
The years shall ne'er destroy our love,
But only give us change of bliss.

Had I a wish? it's all for thee:
I know thy wish is me to please:
Our moments pass so smooth away,
That other folks look on and gaze;
Well pleased to see our happy days,
Envy's self has naught to blame,
Thy bosom still shall be my hame.

I'll lay me there and take my rest:
And if that should disturb my dear,
I'd bid her laugh her cares away,
And bid her not to shed a tear.
Have I a joy? it's all for thee;
United still your heart and mine;
They're like the ivy round the tree,
That's twined till death shall them disjoin.

## EPISTLE TO JOHN LAPRAIK

An Old Scottish Bard.

April 1, 1785.

While briers and woodbines budding green,
With partridge screeching loud at e'en,
And jumping hares on meadows seen,
    Inspire my muse,
This freedom in an unknown friend,
    I pray excuse.

To socialise we had a meeting,
To talk with folks and do some singing,
We had such hearty fun and joking,
    You need not doubt;
And then we had a bout of laughing,
    And fell about.

There was one song, above the rest,
Among them all it pleased me best,
That some kind husband had addressed,
    To some sweet wife:
It touched the heart-strings through the breast,
    So true to life.

I've scarce heard ought described so weel
What generous manly bosoms feel;
Thought I, 'can this be Pope, or Steele
    Or Beattie's work?'
They told me 'twas a man who dwells
    About Muirkirk.

It overwhelmed me just to hear it,
And so about him I enquired;
And all that knew him then declared it,
    He was sublime;
That none excelled him, few came near him,
    In prose or rhyme.

So, set him to a pint of ale,
And let him say a merry tale,
Or rhymes or songs he'd made himsel',
    Or witty catches,
'Tween Inverness and Teviot dale,
    He had few matches.

Then up I got and swore an oath,
That I would pawn my plough and cloth,
Or die a broken pony's death,
    In some dyke back;
A pint and gill I'd give them both,
    To hear your talk.

But, first and foremost, I should tell,
Almost as soon as I could spell,
I to the rhyming jingle fell,
    Though rude and rough;
Yet crooning to a body's sel',
    Does well enough.

I am no poet, in a sense,
But just a rhymer, just by chance,
And have to learning no pretence,
    Yet what the matter?
Whene'er my muse does on me glance,
    I jingle at her.

Your critic folk may cock their nose,
And say, 'How can you e'er propose,
You, who know hardly verse from prose
    To make a song?'
But, by your leaves, my learned foes,
    You're maybe wrong.

What's all your jargon of your schools,
Your Latin names for horns and stools;
If honest nature made you fools,
    What of your grammars?
You've better use of spades and tools,
    And big sledge-hammers.

A set of dull conceited blockheads
Confuse their brains in college classes.
They go in pups and come out asses,
  Plain truth to speak;
And then they think to climb Parnassus,
  With little Greek.

Give me one spark of nature's fire,
That's all the learning I desire;
Then, though I trudge through muck and mire
  With plough or cart,
My muse, though homely in attire,
  May touch the heart.

Oh for a touch of Allen's joy,                    *Ramsey.*
Or Fergusson's, the bold and sly,
Or bright Lapraik's, my friend to be,
  If I can hit it.
Their learning is enough for me,
  If I could get it.

Now, sir, if all your friends be true,
Though real friends I believe are few,
Your list of friends I'd join it too,
  If you'll permit.
And if you want a friend that's new,
  I'm not unfit.

I would not boast about mysel':
As ill I like my faults to tell,
But friends and folk that know me well,
  They sometimes praise me,
Though I must own, there's many more,
  Who do abuse me.

There's one small fault, for which they blame me
I like the lasses – God forgive me,
For many's the pence they've wheedled from me,
  At dance or fair;
Maybe some other thing they'd give me,
  That they can spare.

At Mauchline race, or Mauchline fair,
I should be proud to meet you there;
We'll have a night that's free from care,
    If we forgather,
And have a swap of rhyming ware
    With one another.

The two pint toper? let him natter.
We'll christen him with dirty water,
And then we'll drink, talk, and chatter
    To cheer our heart;
And faith, we'll be acquainted better,
    Before we part.

There's nothing like good honest nappy;     *Ale.*
Where will you see a man so happy,
Or women soft, and sweet, and sappy,
    'Tween morn and morn,
As them that like to take a drappie,     *Drop.*
    In glass or horn?

I've seen me dazed upon a time.
I scarce could wink these eyes of mine,
Then one half-pint just does me fine,
    It gives me life,
Then back I rattle on the rhyme,
    As keen's a knife.

Away you selfish worldly race,
Who think that style, sense, and grace,
E'en love and friendship, should give place
    To filthy lucre.
I do not like to see your face,
    It's like a cancer.

But you whom social pleasure charms,
Whose hearts the tide of kindness warms,
Who hold your being on the terms,
    'Each aid the others,'
Come to my bowl, come to my arms,
    My friends, my brothers.

But, to conclude my long epistle,
My old pen's coming to a frazzle,
Two lines from you would make me sizzle,
    Who am, most fervant,
While I can either sing or whistle,
    Your friend and servant.

# SECOND EPISTLE TO LAPRAIK

## April 21, 1785.

Unfortunately Lapraiks replies to the three epistles are not extant.

When new-calfed cows pull at the stake,          *Tethered.*
And ponies sweat as if to break,
This hour on evening's edge I take,
  To own I'm debtor
To honest hearted, old Lapraik,
  For his kind letter.

Worn and tired with weary legs,
Sowing the corn out o'er the rigs,          *Fields.*
Or tending to the thirsty nags,
  Their ten-hour bite,
My awkward Muse sore pleads and begs,
  I could not write.

The free and feckless thoughtless hussy,
She's soft at best, and somewhat lazy,
Quoth she, 'You know we've been so busy
  This month and more,
That, truth, my head is grown right dizzy,
  And something sore.'

Her daft excuses make me mad,
'Conscience,' says I, 'you thoughtless maid,
I'll write, and you will be repaid,
  This very night;
So don't you ever affront your trade,
  But rhyme it right.

Shall bold Lapraik, the king of hearts,
Though mankind was but a pack of cards,
Praise you so well for your deserts,
  In terms so friendly,
Yet you'll neglect to show your parts,
  And thank him kindly?'

So, given time to sit and think,
I dipped my pen into the ink,
Quoth I, 'Before I sleep a wink,
        I vow I'll close it,
And if the rhyming lacks the link,
        By Jove I'll prose it.'

So I've began to scrawl – but whether,
In rhyme or prose, or both together,
Or some hotch-potch that's rightly neither,
        Let time make proof,
But I shall scribble down some blether;
        Of that forsooth.

My worthy friend, ne'er grudge or carp,
Though Fortune use you hard and sharp,
Come, tickle up your moorland harp
        With gleesome touch,
Ne'er mind how Fortune waft and warp,
        She's but a bitch.

She's given me many a jerk and kick,
Never spread my butter thick,
But by the Lord, though I should beg
        In my old age,
I'll laugh, and sing, and shake a leg,
        Before I'll rage.

Now comes my six and twentieth summer,
I've seen the buds upon the timber.
The girls still tear my heart asunder
        From year to year
And though I flirt, frisk, and flounder,
        I, Rob, am here.

Do you envy city gents?
Behind a counter counting cents,
Proud of profits so immense,
        They bloat his belly?
An awful sight, he represents,
        Mankind's folly.

Or, is't the haughty feudal Thane,
With fancy shirt and gold-knobbed cane,
Who passes wide the lowly train,
    And lordly stalks,
While caps and bonnets off are ta'en,
    As by he walks?

O Thou who gives us each good gift,
Give me of wit and sense a lift,
Then turn me, if thou please, adrift,
    Through Scotland wide.
With Lord or Lairds I would not mix,
    In all their pride.

Were this the charter of our state,
'On pain of Hell be rich and great',
Damnation then would be our fate,
    Beyond remead;
But, thanks to Heaven, that's not the gate,          *Way.*
    We learn our creed.

For thus the royal mandate ran,
When first the human race began,
'The social, friendly, honest man,
    Whate're he be,
'Tis he fulfils great nature's plan,
    And none but he'.

O mandate glorious and divine,
The ragged followers of the Nine,          *Muses.*
Poor, thoughtless devils, yet may shine
    In glorious light,
While sordid sons of Mammon's line,
    Are dark as night.

Though here they scrape, and squeeze and growl,
Their worthless handful of a soul,
May in some future carcase howl,
    The forest's fright,
Or in some day-detesting owl
    May shun the light.

Then may Lapraik and Burns arise,
To reach their native kindred skies,
And sing their pleasures, hopes and joys,
        In some mild sphere,
Still closer knit in friendship's ties,
        Each passing year.

# THIRD EPISTLE TO JOHN LAPRAIK

## Sept. 13, 1785.

Written between showers of rain at harvest time.

God speed you further on my Johnnie
Good health, firm hands, and weather bonny;
And may you never want for many
   Loaves of bread,
And never lack a glass of brandy
   To clear your head.

May northern winds ne'er do your threshing,
Nor give your stookéd sheaves a thrashing,
Bringing to naught a twelvemonth's working
   Upon your farm.
May each grain, e'en from the gleaning,
   Come to your barn.

I'm busy too and working at it,
But bitter northern winds have wet it,    *The harvest.*
So I lift my quill and trim it
   And set to work,
To compose a letter of remit,
   Like any clerk.

It's now two months since I'm your debtor,
For your kindly, nameless, dateless letter,
Upbraiding me for harsh ill-nature,
   On holy men,
While Devil take me, you're no better,
   And more profane.

But let the church-folk ring their bells,
Let's sing about our noble sel's;
We want no help from Grecian hills,    *Inspiration.*
   To arouse us,
But landlord's wives, and whisky stills,
   They are the muses.

Your friendship, sir, I will not quit it,
And if you make objections to it,
Then hand in hand some day we'll bind it,
        And witness take,
And with some whisky Scotch cement it.
        It will not break.

When horse and harness can be spared,
And cattle do not need a herd
And all the corn-stacks in the yard
        Are tied down tight,
I mean your fireside to guard,
        One winter night.

Then muse-inspiring Scottish whisky,
Shall make us both so wise and witty,
Till you forget your old and gouty
        And well nigh sixty,
And act like nine years less than thirty,
        Sweet one and twenty.

Now all the stooks are downward cast,
The sun is shining in the west,
And I must run among the rest
        And quit my banter,
So I subscribe myself in haste,
        Yours, Rab the Ranter.

# ON SCARING SOME WATERFOWL ON LOCH TURIT

There is no record of Burns being a 'hunting, shooting, fishing man'. On the contrary, he appears to abhor such sport and several of his poems reflect this. As the Wee Mousie ran away from him, so he ponders why the wild duck take flight at his presence.

Why, ye tenants of the lake,
For me your watery haunt forsake?
Tell me, fellow creatures, why
At my presence thus you fly?
Why disturb your social joys,
Parent, filial, kindred ties?
Common friend to you and me,
Nature's gifts to all are free:
Peaceful keep your dimpling wave,
Busy feed, or wanton lave;
Or, beneath the sheltering rock,
Bide the surging billow's shock.


Conscious, blushing for our race,
Soon, too soon, your fears I trace.
Man, your proud, usurping foe,
Would be lord of all below:
Plumes himself in Freedom's pride,
Tyrant stern to all beside.


The eagle, from the cliffy brow,
Marking you his prey below,
In his breast no pity dwells,
Strong necessity compels;
But man, to whom alone is given
A ray direct from pitying Heaven,
Glories in his heart humane –
And creatures for his pleasure slain.

In these savage, liquid plains,
Only known to wandering swains,
Where the mossy riv'let strays
Far from human haunts and ways,
All on nature you depend,
And life's poor season peaceful spend.

Or, if man's superior might
Dare invade your native right,
On the lofty ether borne,
Man with all his powers you scorn;
Swiftly seek on clanging wings,
Other lakes and other springs;
And the foe you cannot brave,
Scorn at least to be his slave.

## THE BLUE EYED LASS

The young lady to whom Burns pays such compliments was Miss Jean Jeffrey, who bestowed her charms, within matrimony, to an American, a Mr. Renwick.

I wandered wayward and unwise,
A way I fear I'll dearly rue,
I got my death from two sweet eyes,
Two lovely eyes of bonny blue.
'Twas not her golden ringlets bright,
Nor lips like roses wet with dew,
Nor heaving bosom, lily white –
It was her eyes of bonny blue.

She talked, she smiled, my heart she wiled;
She charmed my soul I know not how,
But oh the wound, the deadly wound,
Came from her eyes of bonny blue.
She would not speak, nor yet say no,
Perhaps she'll listen to my view;
Should she refuse, to death I'll go,
For those two eyes of bonny blue.

## WHEN FIRST I SAW FAIR JEANIE'S FACE

This is a sequel to 'The Blue Eyed Lass'. Although composed in 1790, it's first publication was in *The New York Mirror* in 1846.

When first I saw fair Jeanie's face
I could not tell what ailed me;
My heart went flittering pit-a-pat,
My eyes they almost failed me.
She's always neat, so trim, so bright,
All grace does round her hover;
One look deprived me of my heart,
And I became her lover.

Had I Dundas's whole estate,
Or Hopetown's wealth to shine in,
Did warlike laurel crown my brow,
Or humbler leaves entwining –
I'd lay them all at Jeanie's feet,
Could I but hope to move her,
And prouder than a belted knight,
I'd be my Jeanie's lover.

Alas I fear some happier swain,
Has gained my Jeanie's favour:
If so, may every bliss be hers,
Though I may never have her;
Should she go east, should she go west,
'Twixt Forth and Tweed all over,
While men have eyes, or ears, or taste,
She'll always find a lover.

## ELEGY ON THE YEAR 1788

For lords and kings I do not mourn,
Just let them die – for that they're born,
But oh, prodigious to reflect,
A twelvemonth, sirs, have gone to wreck.
O eighty eight in thy small place,
Of what enjoyments you have reft us,
In what a pickle thou has left us.
The Spanish empire's lost a head,
And my old toothless dog is dead;
The struggles sore 'tween Pitt and Fox,          *Statesmen.*
And 'tween my good wife's fighting cocks;
The one is game, a bloody devil;
But to the hen birds not uncivil;
The other's somewhat stiff from treading,
But better bird ne'er scratched a midden.          *Dung heap.*


You ministers preach and hold discourse,
And cry and thump till you are hoarse;
For eighty eight he wished you well,
And gave you both good cloth and meal,
Many a shilling and many a peck,
And yet yourself near came a wreck.


You bonny lasses wipe your eyes,
For some of you have lost a prize,
And gave, from what you should refrain,
What you can never give again.


Observe the cattle and the sheep,
How woe and weary now they creep.
Even the earth itself does cry,
And all the wells are going dry.

O eighty nine, thou's but a bairn,
And not too old, I hope, to learn.
Thou beardless boy, I pray take care,
You now have got your father's chair;
No handcuffed, muzzled, half-shackled regent,          *Prince.*
But, like yourself, a full free agent.
Be sure to follow out your plan
No worse than he did, honest man,          *George III.*
But do much better if you can.

                    Jan. 1st 1789

## THE DISCREET HINT

Lass, when your mother is from home,
Might I but be so bold
As come to your bower window,
And creep in from the cold?
As come to your bower window,
And when it's cold and wet,
Warm me to thy bosom,
Fair lass, will you do that?

Young man, if you should be so bold,
When my mother's far from home,
To come to my bower window,
When I am all alone;
To warm you to my bosom;
But I will tell you what,
The way to me lies through the church,
Young man, do you hear that?

## JOHN ANDERSON, MY JO

John Anderson, my jo John,
When we were first aquent,
Your locks were like the ravens,
Your bonny brow was brent.                    *Smooth.*
But now your crown is bald, John,
Your locks are like the snow,
But blessings on your hoary head,
John Anderson, my jo.

John Anderson, my jo John,
We climbed the hill together,
And many a happy day, John,
We've had with one another.
Now we must totter down, John,
And hand in hand we'll go,
And sleep together at the foot,
John Anderson, my jo.

# WRITTEN IN FRIARS' CARSE HERMITAGE

Burns had the freedom to roam at will the sylvan settings of Friars' Carse Hermitage where he inscribed the first lines on a pane of glass.

Thou whom chance may hither lead,
Be thou clad in russet weed,
Be thou decked in silken stole,
Grave these maxims on thy soul:-

Life is but a day at most,
Sprung from night, in darkness lost;
Hope not sunshine every hour,
Fear not clouds will always lour.

As Youth and Love, with sprightly dance,
Beneath thy morning star advance,
Pleasure, with her siren air,
May delude the thoughtless pair;
Let Prudence bless Enjoyment's cup,
Then rapture sip, and sip it up.

As thy day grows warm and high,
Life's meridian flaming nigh,
Dost thou spurn the humble vale?
Life's proud summits wouldst thou scale?
Check thy climbing step, elate;
Evils lurk in felon wait;
Dangers, eagle-pinioned, bold,
Soar around each cliffy hold;
While cheerful Peace, with linnet song,
Chants the lowly dells among.

As the shades of evening close,
Beck'ning thee to long repose;
As life itself becomes disease,
Seek the chimney-nook of ease,
There ruminate with sober thought
On all thou'st seen, and heard, and wrought;
And teach the sportive youngsters round

Saws of experience, sage and sound.
Say, Man's true, genuine estimate,
The grand criterion of his fate,
Is not, Art thou high or low?
Did thy fortune ebb and flow?
Wast thou cottager or king?
Peer or peasant? – no such thing.
Did many talents gild thy span?
Or frugal Nature grudge thee one?
Tell them, and press it on their mind.
As thou thyself must shortly find,
The smile or frown of awful Heaven
To virtue or to vice is given.
Say, to be just, and kind, and wise,
There solid self-enjoyment lies;
That foolish, selfish, faithless ways,
Lead to the wretched, vile and base.

Thus resigned and quiet creep
To the bed of lasting sleep –
Sleep, whence thou shalt ne'er awake;
Night, where dawn shall never break;
Till future life, future no more,
To light and joy the good restore,
To light and joy unknown before.

Stranger, go; Heaven be thy guide;
Quoth the beadsman of Nith-side.                    *R.B.*

*Beadsman – a recipient of charity.*

## CONTENTED WITH LITTLE

Contented with little but happy with more,
When over my troubles I nightly pore,
I give them a whack as they creep along,
With a pint of good ale and an old Scottish song.

My thoughts often land me in troublesome plight,
But man is a soldier and life is a fight;
My mirth and good humour are coin in my pouch,
The freedom I worship no monarch dare touch.

A twelvemonth of trouble, should that be my fall,
A night of good-fellowship soon sweetens the gall.
When at the blythe end of our journey at last,
Who the devil ever thinks of the road that is past?

Blind chance ever stumbles and strays,
Never mind, let the jade have her ways.
Come ease or travail, come pleasure or pain,
My worst word is – Welcome and welcome again.

## HERE'S TO THY HEALTH MY BONNIE LASS

Here's to thy health my bonnie lass,
Good night, and joy be with you.
I'll come no more to thy bower door,
To tell you that I love you.
Oh do not think my pretty dear,
That I can't live without you.
I vow and swear, I do not care,
How long you look about you.

You were so free informing me
You had no mind to marry.
I'll be so free informing thee
No time have I to tarry.
I know thy friends try every means
From wedlock to delay you,
Depending on some higher chance –
But fortune may betray you.

I know they scorn my low estate,
But that does never grieve me;
But I'm as free as any he.
Small silver will relieve me.
I'll count my health my greatest wealth,
So long as I enjoy it;
I'll get my grant, I'll fear no want,
As long's I get employment.

But far-off fowls have feathers fair,
At least until you try them;
Though they seem fair, still have a care;
They may prove worse than I am.
But at mid-night, when the moon shines bright,
My dear I'll come and see thee;
For the man that loves his mistress well,
No travel makes him weary.

# POEM
## ADDRESSED TO MR. MITCHELL COLLECTOR OF EXCISE
### DUMFRIES, DECEMBER 1795

This poem asking for the loan of £1.05 epitomizes the dire straits his health and finances were in. It is a matter of reproach to his compatriots and Brotherhood. 'He wanted bread and they gave him a stone.' (Monument after his death.)

Friend of the poet, conscious of my weal,
Without thee I must beg or steal,
For alas, the Devil's made me kneel
    Before him and his witches;
I'll be deprived of house and meal,
    And my scanty riches.

I modestly and hereby hinted,
That one pound one I sorely want it,         £1.05.
If with the serving girl you sent it,
    It would be kind;
If you could see your way to lend it,
    And do not mind.

So may the old year go out moaning,
To see the new come laden, groaning
With double plenty every morning
    To thee and thine;
Domestic peace and comforts crowning
    The whole design.

## POSTSCRIPT

You've heard this while how I've been beaten,
And by fell death almost been stricken;
Grim ghoul he had me shaking
        In my bed;
But by good luck, I'm not forsaken,
        I'm still not dead.

But now I've got my share of health,
I'll guard it as I do my wealth,
And take judicious care of it
        Before I'll fall.
Then farewell folly, hide and hair of it,
        One and for all.

## THE BOOK WORMS

   Burns was browsing in some lord's grand library and noted the uncut (therefore unread) leaves, as well as book worms.

Through and through the inspired leaves
Ye maggots make your windings,
But oh respect his lordship's taste,
And his golden bindings.

## CAPTAIN FRANCIS GROSE

Captain Grose was an authorative antiquarian by profession, and a 'Hail fellow well met' by inclination. He it was who prompted Burns to compose 'Tam O' Shanter'. A corpulant man, he died of apoplexy.

Hear, land of cakes, and brother Scots,
From Solway Firth to John O' Groats;
If there's a hole in all your coats
    Then you should mend it:
For Grose is busy taking notes,
    And faith he'll print it.

If in your bounds you chance to light
Upon a fine fat fellow wight,
Of stature short, but genius bright,
    That's him, I warn you –
Beware, for he's an artist with some bite,
    And will portray you.

By some old haunted castle grey,
Or ruined church where witches pray,
It's ten to one he'll come that way,
    For that's his calling.
With devils and such he has much sway;
    That's quite appalling.

Each ghost that haunts old house or chamber,
You gypsy gang that deal in glamour,
And you, deep read in Hell's black grammar,
    Warlocks and witches;
You'll quake at his conjuring hammer,
    You midnight bitches.

It's told he was a soldier bred,
And one that would have never fled:
But now he's quit the bloody blade
    And rifle bullet,
And taken the antiquarian trade,
    I think they call it.

He has a store of old nick-nacks,
Rusty iron by the sacks,
To make enough of cobbler's nails
    For all the county;
And porridge pots and milk-maids pails,
    Such is his bounty.


Of Eve's first fire he has a cinder,
Of Vulcan's shovel he has a splinter;
And that which distinguished the gender
    Of Balaam's ass;
The broom-stick of the Witch of Endor,
    Well shod with brass.


He'll sell to you, with ne'er a sign of guilt,
Some tartan cloth from Adam's kilt,
The knife that cut poor Abel's throat
    He'll prove to you and say,
'Twas found in seaman Noah's boat,
    And came to him that way.


But you should see him in his glee,
For so much fun and glee has he,
Then set him down with two or three
    Good fellows with him;
Then bring the port and let them be,
    And then you'll see him.


Now, by the powers of verse and prose,
Thou art a crafty dog, O Grose;
But who of thee shall ill suppose,
    They sore miscall thee;
I'd take the rascal by the nose,
    And say 'Shame on thee'.

On a convivial occasion the Captain asked Burns to compose an epitaph to him. This was the impromptu reply:-

The Devil got notice old Grose was a-dying,
So quick at the summons, old Satan came flying;
But when he approached where poor Francis lay moaning,
And saw each bed-post with its burden a-groaning,
Astonished, confounded, cried Satan, 'By God
Although I do want him, I can't bear the load.'

## MAUCHLINE BELLES

Don't read such novels, Mauchline belles,
Your safer at your spinning wheels.
Such witching books are baited hooks,
For rakish rooks – like Rob Mossgiel.                    *R.B.*

The authors lewd and printers crude,
They make your youthful fancies reel.
They heat your veins, and fire your brains,
And then you're prey – for Rob Mossgiel.

Beware a tongue that's smoothly hung,
A heart that warmly seems to feel.
That feeling heart but acts the part,
'Tis rakish art – in Rob Mossgiel.

The frank address, the soft caress,
Are worse than poisoned darts of steel.
The frank address, and politeness,
Are all finesse – in Rob Mossgiel.

## THE JOLLY BEGGARS

This amusing poem describes how outcasts from Society escape from reality, and a cold winter's night, by carousing in a lowly tavern. It is also a record of military and social history.

Recitation

When autumn leaves bestrew the yard,
Or, wavering like a baukie bird,                    *Bat.*
Fend off the north's cold blast;
When hailstones drive away the light,
And infant frosts begin to bite,
In early hoar-frost dressed,
One night, at e'en a merry corp
Of randy vagrant bodies
In 'Poosie Nansies' held the floor,                 *Tavern.*
And drank away their follies:
With quaffing and laughing,
They ranted and they sang,
With jumping and thumping,
The very pots all rang.


First, next the fire, in old red rags               *Old uniform.*
He sat beside his victual bags,
And knapsack all in order;
His doxy lay within his arm;
With whisky raw and blankets warm
She swooned upon her soldier;
She always gives the shy 'come on'
While waiting for his kiss,
While holding up her ready mouth,
Just like a big alms dish.
Their kisses resounded,
Just like a carter's whip,
Then staggering and swaggering,
He roared this ditty up:-

## Song

I am a son of Mars, who has been in many wars,
And show my cuts and scars wherever I come.
This here was for a wench, and this other in a trench,
When welcoming the French, at the sound of the drum.

My 'prenticeship I passed, when my leader breathed
              his last,                                        *Gen. Wolfe.*
When the bloody die was cast, on the heights of Abraham.
I servéd out my trade, when the gallant game was played,
And the Moro low was laid, at the sound
              of the drum.                                     *Cuban fort.*

I served with Captain Curtis, 'mong the floating
              batteries,                                       *Gibraltar.*
And there I left for witness an arm and a leg,
Yet let my Country need me, and with Elliot to lead me,
I'd clatter on my stumps at the sound of the drum.

And now though I must beg, with a wooden arm and leg,
And many a tattered rag hanging over my bum,
I'm as happy to be here, with my woman and my beer,
As when I dressed in scarlet, to follow the drum.

What though with hoary locks, I must stand the winter's
              shocks,
Beneath the woods and rocks, where oft I dwell
With my trading I'll do well, and letting out a yell,
I could meet a troop from Hell, at the sound of a drum.

## Recitation

As he ended rafters shook
Above the chorus roar,
And frightened rats with backward look
Made for the open door.
A fiddler next then took the floor
And fiddled out a loud 'encore',
But up arose the martial crowd,
And stopped the loud uproar.

## Song

I once was a maid though I cannot tell when,
And still my delight is in proper young men.
Someone of a troop of Dragoons was my daddie,
No wonder I'm fond of my soldier laddie.

The first of my loves was a swaggering blade,
To rattle the thundering drum was his trade;
His leg was so tight, and his cheek was so ruddy,
Transported I was with my soldier laddie.

But the godly old chaplain left him in the lurch;
The sword I forsook for the sake of the church;
He ventured his soul, and I risked my body;
'Twas then I proved false to my soldier laddie.

Full soon I grew sick of my sanctified lot.
The Regiment at large for a husband I got;
From the gilded spontoon to the fife I was ready,    *Battle-axe.*
I asked for no more than a fine soldier laddie.

But peace it reduced me to beg in despair,
Till I met my old boy at Cunningham fair;
His rags regimental they fluttered so gaudy,
My heart it rejoiced at my soldier laddie.

And now I have lived – I know not how long,
And still can join in a cup or a song;
But with both hands I can hold a glass steady,
Here's to thee, my hero, my soldier laddie.

## Recitation

Poor merry Andrew in the nook
Sat drinking with his hussy.
They minded neither leer nor look
For between themselves were busy.
At length with drink and courting dizzy
He staggered up with grave grimace.
Yet still he kissed his hussy,
Then tuned his pipes till red in face.

## Song

Sir Wisdom's a fool I do vow.
Sir Knave is a fool in a session.
He's there but a 'prentice I trow,
But I am a fool by profession.


My grannie she bought me a book,
And I went away to the school.
I fear I my talent mistook,
But what will you have for a fool?


For drink I would venture my neck,
And wenching is half of my craft,
But what would you or other expect,
Of one that's avowedly daft?


I once felt the sting of the birch,
For noisily swearing and quaffing.
I once was rebuked in the church
For fondling a lass in my daffin.                    *Fun.*


Poor Andrew who tumbles for sport
Let nobody name with a jeer.
There's even, I'm told, in the Court
A tumbler called the Premier.


Observe you, yon reverend lad                       *Priest.*
Makes faces to tickle the mob.
He rails at our mountebank squad;
We're rivals to him and his job.


And now my conclusion I'll tell;
For faith I'm confoundedly dry.
The man that's a fool for himsel',
Good Lord, he's far dafter than I.

## Recitation

Then next outspoke a sturdy old dame.
Collection of money was her best game,
For many's the pockets she's picked,
And in many a pond has been ducked.
Her love had been for a wayward drifter,
But now he has worn the final halter.          *Hanged.*
With sighs and sobs she thus began
To wail her wayward strong young man.

## Song

A Highland lad my love was born.
The Lowland laws he held in scorn,
But still was faithful to his clan:
My gallant braw John Highlandman.

> Sing, hey my braw John Highlandman,
> Sing, ho, my braw John Highlandman.
> There's not a lad in all the land
> Was match for my John Highlandman.

With tartan kilt, and tartan plaid,
And trusty sword down by his side,
The ladies' hearts he did trepan,
My gallant braw John Highlandman.

We ranged the Land from Tweed to Spey,
And lived like lords and ladies gay,
For a lowland face he feared not one;
My gallant braw John Highlandman.

They banished him beyond the sea
But ere the bud was on the tree
Adown my cheek the pearlies ran,
Embracing my John Highlandman.

But, Oh, they caught him at the last,
And bound him in a dungeon fast.
My curse upon them everyone:
They've hanged my braw John Highlandman.

And now a widow, I must mourn
The pleasures that will ne'er return.
No comfort but a hearty can,
When I think on John Highlandman.


### Recitation


A pigmy scraper with his fiddle,
At fairs and markets used to driddle;                    *Play.*
But fleshy thighs and buxom middle,
    (He reached no higher),
Had holed his heart just like a riddle,
    And set on fire.


With hand on hip and upward e'e
He crooned his gamut, one, two, three,
Then in an ariosa key,
    The wee Apollo
Set off with allegretto glee
    His fulsome solo.


### Song


Let me reach up and wipe that tear,
And come with me and be my dear,
And then your every care and fear
May whistle for the rest of it.

    I am a fiddler to my trade,
    And all the tunes I ever played,
    The sweetest still to wife and maid
    Was whistle o'er the rest of it.

At wakes and weddings we'll be there,
And oh, so nicely we will fare.
We'll rant and drink till Daddie Care
Sings Whistle o'er the rest of it.

We'll gnaw at bones just like a tyke,
And sun ourselves about the dyke,                                    *dog.*
And at our leisure when we like,
We'll whistle for the rest of it.

But bless me with your heaven of charms,
While with my fiddle beg for alms.
Hunger, cold, and all such harms
May whistle and be spared of it.

### Recitation

Her charms had struck a sturdy tinker.
(And also too our poor gut-scraper.)                              *Fiddler.*
He threw a challenge to our fiddler,
And then he drew a rusty rapier.

He swore for all that he was worth
To split him like a plover,
Unless he would from this time forth
Relinquish her for ever.

With runny eyes and many sighs
Upon his knees descended,
And prayed for grace with rueful face,
And so the quarrel ended.
But though the little heart did grieve
When round the tinker pressed her,
He feigned to laugh into his sleeve
When the tinker thus addressed her:–

### SONG

My bonny lass I work in brass,
A tinker is my station.
I've travelled round all Christian ground
In this my occupation.
I've taken gold, I've been enrolled
In many a noble squadron;
In vain they searched, when off I marched,
To patch a leaking cauldron.

Despise that shrimp, that withered imp,
With all his noise and capering,
And take a share with those that bear,
The tool-bag and the apron.
And by that glass and faith, my lass,
And by this good old whisky,
If e'er you want, or meet with scant,
I'll never be far from you.


## Recitation

The tinker won, the unblushing pair,
In tight embraces sunk;
Partly overcome with love so fair,
And partly she was drunk.
Sir Violina with an air
That showed a man of spunk,
Wished unison upon the pair,
And made the bottle clink
  To their health that night.

But lurking Cupid shot a shaft
That played the dame a trick.
The fiddler laid her fore and aft
Abaft the barley rick.
Her lord, a wight on poet's craft,
Though limping with an injury,
He trailed around with gait so daft,
But still made music merry,
  For all that night.

He was a care-defying blade,
As ever Bacchus listed.
Though fortune sore upon him laid
His heart she never missed it.
He had no wish but to be glad,
No want but when he thirsted,
He hated nought but to be sad,
And thus the muse suggested
  His song that night.

## Song

I am a bard of no regard,
To gentle folk and all that,
But bold or cowed, the staring crowd,
Do welcome me and all that.

> For all that and all that,
> And twice as much as all that,
> I've lost but one, I've two behind;
> I've wife enough for all that.

I never drank where muses thirst
Of Grecian streams and all that.
But here it's pure, and not the worst;
My Helicon I call that.                    *Poet's Grecian abode.*

Great love I bear to all the fair,
Their humble slave and all that,
But lordly will I hold it still
A mortal sin to thwart that.

In raptures sweet, this hour we meet
With mutual love and all that,
But for how long the bee may sting,
Let inclination law that.

Their tricks and craft have sent me daft,
I've been deceived and all that,
But clear the decks, and here's the sex;
I like the jades for all that.

> For all that and all that,
> And twice as much as all that,
> My dearest blood, to do them good,
> I welcome them to all that.

## Recitation

So sung the bard – and Nancie's walls,
Shook with the thunder of applause,
Re-echoed from each mouth:
They emptied pockets, pawned their clothes,
To free themselves of this world's woes,
And quench their burning thirst.
Then over again the jovial throng
The poet did request
To drop his pack and sing a song,
A ballad of the best.
He rising, rejoicing,
Between his two Deborahs,
Looks round him, and found them,
Impatient for his chorus.


## Song

See the smoking bowl before us
Mark our jovial ragged ring.
Round and round take up the chorus,
And in raptures let us sing.

    A fig for those by law protected.
    Liberty's a glorious feast.
    Courts for cowards were erected.
    Churches built to please the priest.

What is title? What is treasure?
What is reputation's care?
If we lead a life of pleasure,
'Tis no matter how or where.

With a ready trick and fable,
Round we wander all the day,
And at night in barn or stable,
Hug our doxies in the hay.

Does the train-attended carriage
Through the country lighter rove?
Does the sober bed of marriage
Witness brighter scenes of love?

Life is all a variorum.
We regard not how it goes.
Let them cant about decorum
Who have characters to lose.

Here's to all we have in common.
Here's to all our wandering train.
Here's our ragged brats and women.
One and all cry out – Amen.

## A MOTHER'S LAMENT
### For the death of her son.

Fate gave the word, the arrow sped,
And pierced my darling's heart,
And with him all the joys are fled,
Life can to me impart.
By cruel hands the sapling drops,
In dust dishonoured laid;
So fell the pride of all my hopes,
My agéd future's Shade.

The mother bird surveys her nest,
Bewails the ravished young;
So I, within my aching breast,
Lament the live-day long.
Death, oft I've feared thy fatal blow,
Now fond I bare my breast.
Oh, do thou kindly lay me low
With him I love, at rest.

## AULD LANG SYNE
(Old Long Since)

This is the song, sung by millions throughout the world on New Year's Eve, that alone would have made Robert Burns famous. Some of the millions, alas, will be unaware of its source.

Should old acquaintence be forgot,
And never brought to mind;
Should old acquaintence be forgot,
And days of old lang syne.

For old lang syne, my dear,
For old lang syne,
We'll take a cup of kindness yet,
For old lang syne.

We two have run about the hills,
And pulled the daisies fine.
We've wandered many a weary foot,
Since old lang syne.

We two have paddled in the burn,                    *Stream.*
From morning sun till dine,
But seas between us broad have roared,
Since old lang syne.

And here's a hand my trusty friend,
And put your hand in mine.
We'll take a right good willie-waught,              *Drink.*
For old lang syne.

And surely you'll lift up your glass,
For surely I'll lift mine,
And we'll drink a cup of kindness yet,
For old lang syne.

## TAM GLEN

My heart is a-breaking, dear tittie;
Some counsel unto me come len;
To anger them a' is a pity,
But what will I do wi' Tam Glen?

I'm thinking wi' sic a braw fellow
In poortith I might make a fen;
What care I in riches to wallow,
If I maunna marry Tam Glen?

There's Lowrie, the laird o' Drumeller,
'Gude day to you, brute,' he comes ben;
He brags and he blaws o' his siller,
But when will he dance like Tam Glen?

My minnie does constantly deave me,
And bids me beware o' young men;
They flatter, she says, to deceive me, –
But wha can think sae o' Tam Glen?

My daddie says, gin I'll forsake him,
He'll gi'e me guid hunder marks ten,
But if it's ordained I maun take him,
O wha will I get but Tam Glen?

Yestreen at the Valentine's dealing
My heart to my mou' gi'ed a sten;
For thrice I drew ane without failing,
And thrice it was written – Tam Glen.

The last Halloween I was waukin'
My droukit sark-sleeve, as ye ken;
His likeness cam' up the house staukin',
And the very gray breaks o' Tam Glen.

Come, counsel, dear tittie; don't tarry –
I'll gi'e my bonnie black hen,
Gif ye will advise me to marry
The lad I lo'e dearly, Tam Glen.

## TAM GLEN (English version)

My heart is confused in its duty;
Some counsel I want about men,
To anger them all is a pity,
But what will I do with Tam Glen?

I'm thinking with such a fine fellow,
In poverty I might make a frien',
I care not in riches to wallow,
For I want to marry Tam Glen.

There's Lowrie the laird of Drummeller,
He bores and sickens me when
He brags and he boasts of his silver,
But when will he dance like Tam Glen?

My mother does constantly warn me,
And bids me beware of young men;
They flatter, she says, to deceive me,
But who can think that of Tam Glen?

My father says if I forsake him,
He'll give me a hundred pounds ten;
But if it's ordained I must marry,
O who will I wed but Tam Glen?

Last night at the Valentine's dancing,
My heart missed a beat now and then,
When thrice I was picked for a partner,
And thrice I was picked by Tam Glen.

The last Halloween I was drying
Wet clothes by the fire you ken,
When a shadow came through the steam rising,
With the handsome good looks of Tam Glen.

Come, counsel me someone, don't tarry;
I'll give you my bonny black hen,
If you will advise me to marry,
The lad I love dearly, Tam Glen.

## THE DEUKS DANG O'ER MY DADDY

The bairns gat out wi' an unco shout,
The deuks dang o'er my daddy,
The fien ma care, quo' the ferrie auld wife,
He was but a paidlin' body,
He paidles out, an' he paidles in,
An' he paidles late and early,
Thae seven lang years I ha'e lien by his side,
An' he is but a fusionless carlie.

O haud your tongue, my ferrie auld wife,
O haud your tongue now Nansie,
I've seen the day, and sae ha'e ye,
Ye wadna been sae donsie,
I've seen the day ye buttered my brose,
And cuddled me late and early,
But downa-do's come over me now,
And oh, I find it sairly.

# THE DUCKS HAVE PUSHED OVER MY DADDY
## (English Translation)

The bairns gave out a roaring shout,
The duck's pushed over our daddy,
The devil may care, quoth the fiery old wife,
He is but a waddling body,
He waddles out, and he waddles in,
He waddles late and early,
These seven long years I have lain by his side,
But now it happens so rarely.

O hold your tongue ungrateful old wife,
O hold your tongue my Nancy,
I've seen the day and so have you,
When you always were my fancy;
I've seen the nights we've lain close,
And cuddled late and early,
But now it's all gone I cannot tell where,
And oh I do miss it sorely.

## COUNTRY LASSIE

In simmer, when the hay is mawn,
And corn waved green in ilka field,
While claver blooms white o'er the lea,
And roses blaw in ilka bield,
Blithe Bessie, in the milking shiel,
Says, I'll be wed, come o't what will.
Out spak a dame, in wrinkled eild,
O' guid advisement comes nae ill.


It's ye ha'e wooers mony ane,
And, lassie, ye're but young, ye ken;
Then wait awee, and cannie wale,
A routhie butt, a routhie ben.
There's Johnie o' the Buskie-glen,
Fu'is his barn, fu' is his byre;
Tak this frae me my bonnie hen,
It's plenty beets the luver's fire.


For Johnie o' the Buskie-glen,
I dinna care a single flie;
He lo'es so weel his craps and kye,
He has nae luve to spare for me:
But blithe's the blink o' Robie's ee,
And weel I wat he lo'es me dear;
Ae blink o' him I wad na gie
For Buskie-glen and a' his gear.


O thoughtless lassie, life's a faught;
The canniest gate, the strife is sair;
But aye fu'hant is fechtin' best,
A hungry care's an unco care:
But some will spend, and some will spare,
An' wilfu' folk maun hae their will;
Syne as ye brew, my maiden fair,
Keep kind that ye maun drink the yill.

## COUNTRY LASSIE (English version)

In summer when the hay is mown,
And corn waves brave in bright green flush,
And clover white blooms o'er the lea,
And roses grow from briar bush;
Blythe Bessie at her milking said,
'Whate'er the outcome I'll be wed.'
Out spoke a dame of wrinkled age,
With good advisement of a sage.


'If you have lovers more than one,
When lassie you are still but young;
Then wait awhile and wisely choose;
A well-stocked farm you can't refuse.
There's John of Buskie on your mind;
Full is his barn, and full is his byre.
Take this from me, my girl, and find,
That plenty beats a lover's fire.'


'For Johnie of the Buskie glen,
I do not care a single flea;
He loves so well his crops and kye                    *Cows.*
He has no love to spare for me:
But blythes the blink in Robie's eye,
And well I know he loves me dear:
One blink from him I would not give,
For Buskie glen and all his gear.


'O thoughtless lass, all life's a fight,
The Buskie way you'll better fare.
A hand that's full is your best choice,
For hungry care is woeful care.
But some will spend, and some will spare,
And wilful folk must have their will;
So as you brew my maiden fair,
Perhaps you'll drink more than your fill.'

Oh, gear will buy me rigs o' land,
And gear will buy me sheep and kye;
But the tender heart o' leesome luv
The gowd and silla canna buy.
We may be poor, Robie and I;
Light is the burden luve lays on;
Content and luve bring peace and joy –
What mair ha'e queens upon a throne.

'O, gold will buy me lots of land,
And gold will buy me sheep and kye,
But the tender heart of youthful love
The gold and silver cannot buy:
We may be poor, my Rob and I,
But with him I'll ne'er be alone.
Content and love brings peace and joy.
What more have queens upon a throne?

## O STEER HER UP

O steer her up, and haud her gaun,
Her mither's at the mill, jo;
And gin she winna tak her will, jo.
First shore her wi' a kindly kiss,
And ca'anither gill, jo;
And gin she tak the thing amiss,
E'en let her flyte her fill, jo.

O steer her up, and be na blate;
And gin she tak it ill, jo,
Then lea'e the lassie till her fate,
And time nae langer spill, jo.
Ne'er break your heart for ae rebute,
But think upon it still, jo –
That gin the lassie winna do't,
Ye'll fin' anither will, jo.

## O ROUSE HER UP
### (English Translation)

O rouse her up and hold her tight,
While her mother's at the mill;
And should she be inclined to fight,
Then undermine her will.
First woo her with a gentle kiss,
And with some more to follow;
And if she takes this all amiss,
Then that will be her sorrow.

But try again and don't be shy;
And should she jib you still,
Then leave the lassie high and dry,
And time no longer spill.
Don't break your heart for one rebuff,
But think upon it still,
That if the lassie won't oblige,
You'll find a one that will.

Extracts from a poem by the American poet J.G. Whittier.


## BURNS

On receiving a sprig of heather in blossom.

No more these simple flowers belong
To Scottish maid and lover;
Sown in the common soil of song,
They bloom the wide world over.

Wild heather bells and Robert Burns,
The moorland flower and peasant,
How, at their mention, memory turns
Her pages old and pleasant.

I call to mind the summer day,
The early harvest mowing,
The sky with sun and clouds at play,
And flowers with breezes blowing.

Why dream of lands of gold and pearl,
Of loving knight and lady,
When farmer boy and barefoot girl,
Are wandering there already?

Bees hummed, birds twittered, overhead
I heard the squirrels leaping,
The good dog listened while I read,
And wagged his tail in keeping.

I watched him while in sportive mood,
I read 'The Twa Dogs' story,
And half believed he understood
The poet's allegory.

With clearer eyes I saw the worth
Of life among the lowly;
The Bible at his cotter's hearth
Has made my own more holy.

And if at times an evil strain,
To lawless love appealing,
Broke in upon the sweet refrain
Of pure and healthful feeling.

It died upon the eye and ear,
No inward answer gaining:
No heart had I to see or hear
The discord and the staining.

Let those who never erred forget
His worth, in vain bewailings;
Sweet Soul of Song, I own my debt
Uncancelled by his failings.

Lament who will the ribald line
Which tells his lapse from duty,
How kissed the maddening lips of wine
Or wanton ones of beauty:

Through all his tuneful art, how strong
The human feeling gushes,
The very moonlight of his song
Is warm with smiles and blushes.

1854

## ROBERT BURNS
### By H.W. Longfellow

I see amid the fields of Ayr,
A ploughman, who, in foul or fair,
Sings at his task
So clear, we know not if it is
The laverock's song we hear, or his,
Nor care to ask.

For him the ploughing of those fields
A more ethereal harvest yields
Than sheaves of grain;
Songs flush with purple bloom the rye,
The plover's call, the curlew's cry,
Sing in his brain.

Touched by his hand, the wayside weed
Becomes a flower; the lowliest reed
Beside the stream
Is clothed with beauty; gorse and grass
And heather, where his footsteps pass,
The brighter seem.

He sings of love, whose flame illumes
The darkness of lone cottage rooms;
He feels the force,
The treacherous undertow and stress
Of wayward passions, and no less
The keen remorse.

At moments, wrestling with his fate;
His voice is harsh, but not with hate;
The brush-wood, hung
Above the tavern door, lets fall
Its bitter leaf, its drops of gall
Upon his tongue.

But still the burden of his song
Is love of right, disdain of wrong;
Its master-chords

Are Manhood, Freedom, Brotherhood,
Its discords but an interlude
Between the words.

And then to die so young and leave
Unfinished what he might achieve!
Yet better sure
Is this, than wandering up and down
An old man in a country town,
Infirm and poor.

For now he haunts his native land
As an immortal youth; his hand
Guides every plough;
He sits beside each ingle nook
His voice is in each rushing brook
Each rustling bough.

His presence haunts this room tonight
A form of mingled mist and light
From that far coast.
Welcome beneath this roof of mine!
Welcome! this vacant chair is thine,
Dear guest and ghost.

## Alphabetical Index of Titles